MAP OF THE
Furness Railway

Silver Link Silk Editions

SLP

Exploring the Lake District
with the Furness Railway Tours

David Mather

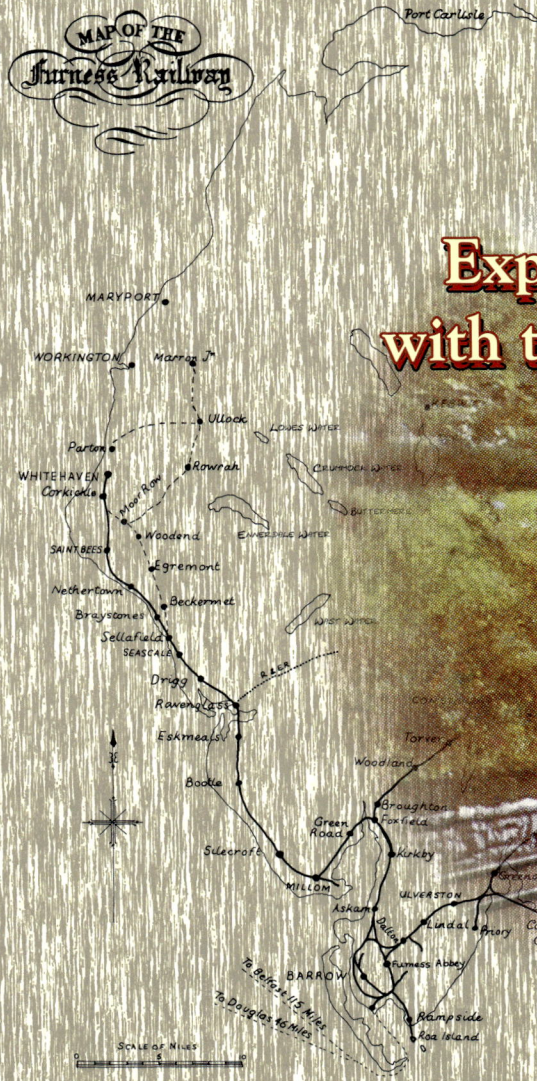

An extract from an 1896 Furness Railway Map

Foreword by Eric Robson

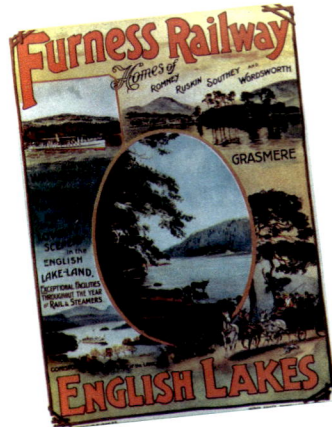

I got into trouble once for saying that any fool can write a guide book – I've written guide books for goodness sake, some of which have made it to other people's bookshelves. David Mather, though, is in an altogether different league. First up, he's an entertaining and informative guide. OK, he's helped by the fact that this is a re-discovered guide book; an evocation of an age of rail travel when companies such as the Furness Railway were discovering that those troublesome customers called passengers could be almost as profitable as the mineral cargoes the railways had been built to carry.

Here, then are twenty tours which were originally designed to encourage Furness passengers to travel further afield; to explore the secret corners of the Lake District. Well researched and beautifully illustrated this fine book sends echoes of those pioneering days into the modern landscapes of Lakeland while cleverly avoiding the worst excesses of trainspotterdom.

So which tour to tackle first?

I may be some time.

Eric Robson

Broadcaster, author, Lakeland farmer
and Chairman of the Wainwright Society

Silver Link Silk Editions

SLP

Exploring the Lake District with the Furness Railway Tours

A guide to exploring the Lake District by retracing the Furness Railway Company's pioneering Circular Tours

David Mather

Silver Link Publishing Ltd

First published in 2015

British Library Cataloguing in Publication Data

A catalogue record for this book is available from the British Library.

Title page: This Tuck's 'Oilette' Famous Expresses Series III postcard circa 1910 shows a Furness Railway 'Lake District Express', with Pettigrew Class 'K2' 4-4-0 No 37 resplendent in 'Indian red' livery in charge of a train of the distinctive 'ultramarine' blue coaches, of which sadly none have survived to be preserved. The reverse of the card reads: 'For Lake Side Station, Windermere, Furness Abbey, Coniston etc., passes through the finest and most picturesque scenery in the country. Along the whole route, charming views present themselves in quick succession to the tourist.'

ISBN 978 185794 441 9

Silver Link Publishing Ltd
The Trundle
Ringstead Road
Great Addington
Kettering
Northants NN14 4BW

Tel/Fax: 01536 330588
email: sales@nostalgiacollection.com
Website: www.nostalgiacollection.com

Printed and bound in the Czech Republic

For my wife Mair, whose help with the manuscript and enthusiastic support during the research have been inspirational.

Special thanks to Eric Robson and Peter Linney of the Wainwright Society, Lakeland Guide David Powell-Thompson, and Sabine Skae at The Dock Museum, Barrow-in-Furness, for their assistance with this project.

All photographs are by the author or from the author's collection unless otherwise stated.

Pre-decimal currency
12 pence = 1 shilling (5p)
240 pence = 20 shillings = £1

IMPORTANT NOTE
The 'Typical journey times' panels are used for illustrative purposes only – the appropriate bus, rail and ferry timetables and service numbers should always be consulted before travelling. Ordnance Survey maps, or a good road atlas for the tours by car, are also recommended.

An extract from an 1896 Furness Railway Map

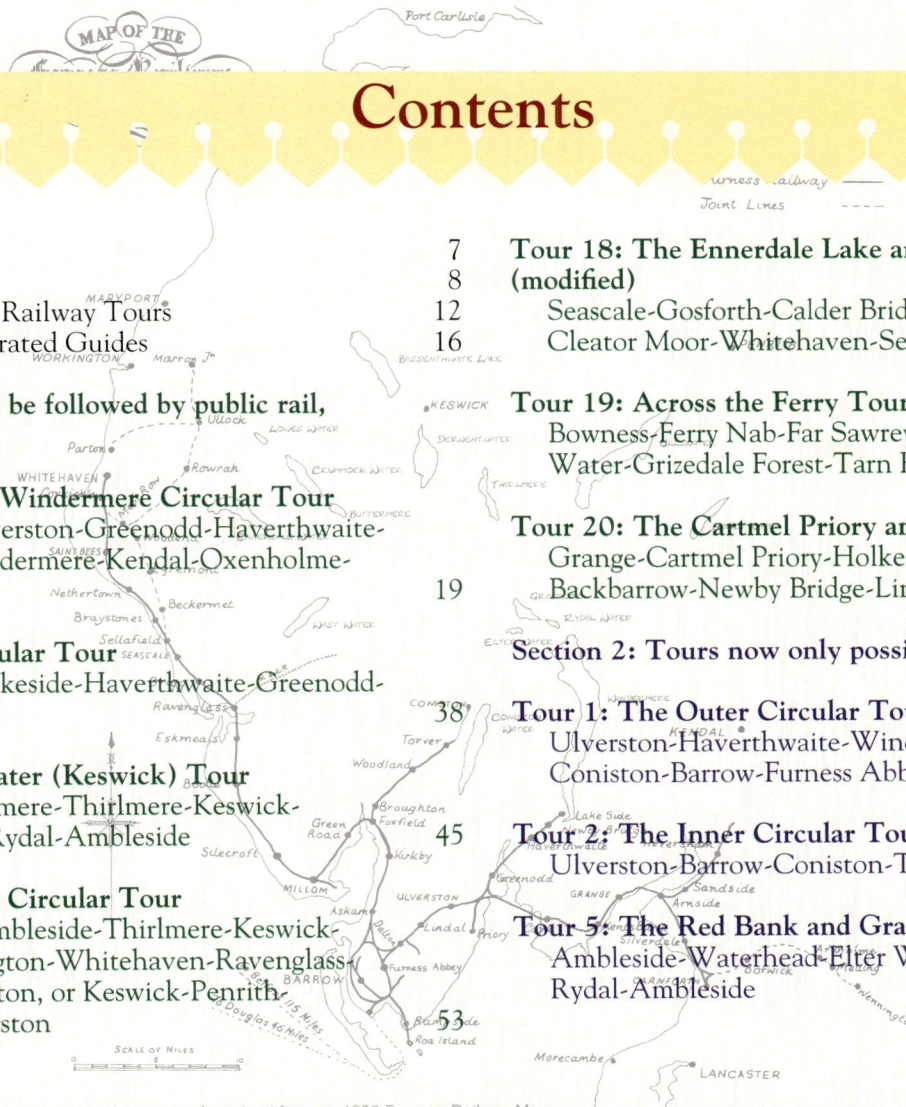

Contents

Bibliography 7

Preface 8

Introduction: The Furness Railway Tours 12

The Furness Railway Illustrated Guides 16

Section 1: Tours that can be followed by public rail, boat and bus services

Tour 3: The Grange and Windermere Circular Tour
Carnforth-Arnside-Ulverston-Greenodd-Haverthwaite-
Lakeside-Bowness-Windermere-Kendal-Oxenholme-
Carnforth 19

Tour 4: The Middle Circular Tour
Ambleside-Bowness-Lakeside-Haverthwaite-Greenodd-
Coniston-Ambleside 38

Tour 12: The Derwentwater (Keswick) Tour
Ambleside-Rydal-Grasmere-Thirlmere-Keswick-
Thirlmere- Grasmere-Rydal-Ambleside 45

Tour 13: The Five Lakes Circular Tour
Ulverston-Lakeside-Ambleside-Thirlmere-Keswick-
Cockermouth-Workington-Whitehaven-Ravenglass-
Millom-Barrow-Ulverston, or Keswick-Penrith-
Tebay-Lancaster-Ulverston 53

**Tour 18: The Ennerdale Lake and Calder Abbey Tour
(modified)**
Seascale-Gosforth-Calder Bridge-Egremont-Moor Row-
Cleator Moor-Whitehaven-Seascale 78

Tour 19: Across the Ferry Tour
Bowness-Ferry Nab-Far Sawrey-Hawkshead-Esthwaite
Water-Grizedale Forest-Tarn Hows-Hawkshead-Bowness 88

Tour 20: The Cartmel Priory and Newby Bridge Tour
Grange-Cartmel Priory-Holker Hall-Haverthwaite-
Backbarrow-Newby Bridge-Lindale-Grange 92

Section 2: Tours now only possible by car

Tour 1: The Outer Circular Tour
Ulverston-Haverthwaite-Windermere-Ambleside-
Coniston-Barrow-Furness Abbey-Ulverston 99

Tour 2: The Inner Circular Tour
Ulverston-Barrow-Coniston-Torver-Greenodd-Ulverston 107

Tour 5: The Red Bank and Grasmere Tour
Ambleside-Waterhead-Elter Water-Red Bank-Grasmere-
Rydal-Ambleside 114

An extract from an 1896 Furness Railway Map

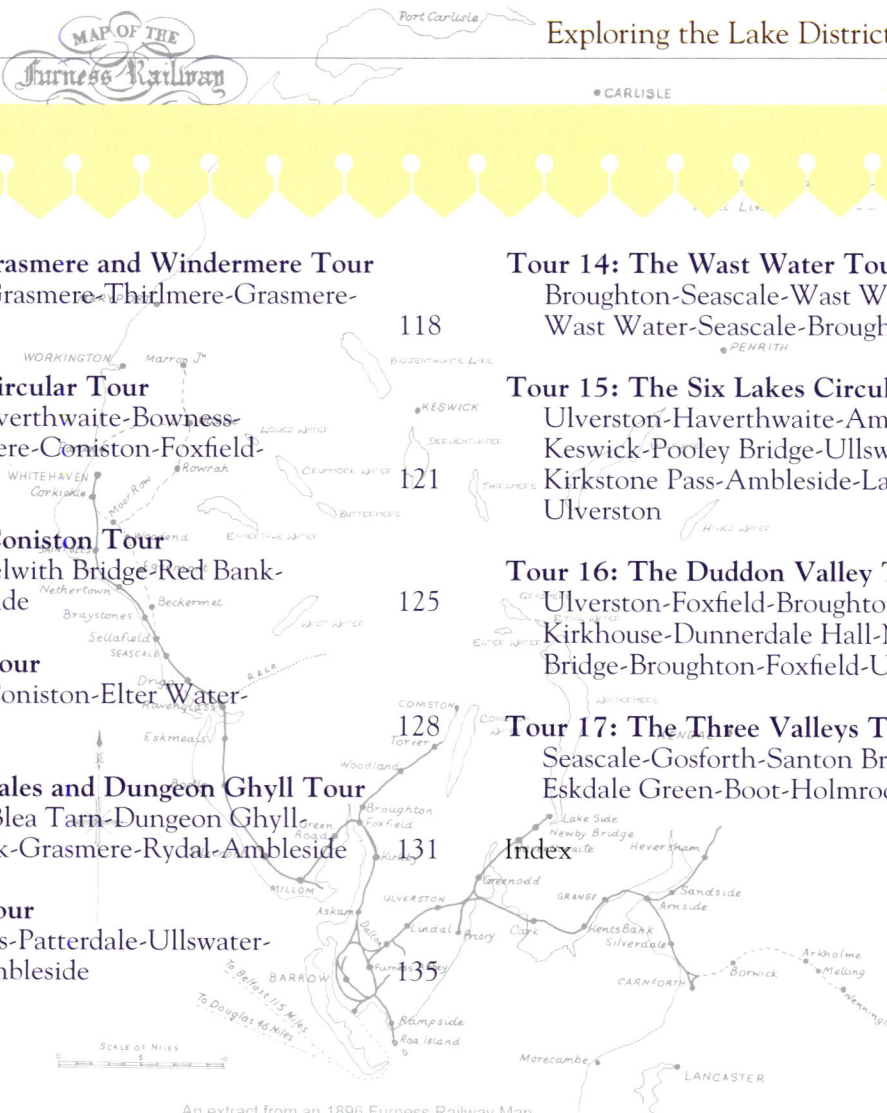

Tour 6: The Thirlmere, Grasmere and Windermere Tour
Ambleside-Waterhead-Grasmere-Thirlmere-Grasmere-
Rydal-Ambleside   118

Tour 7: The Four Lakes Circular Tour
Ulverston-Greenodd-Haverthwaite-Bowness-
Ambleside-Rydal-Grasmere-Coniston-Foxfield-
Barrow-Ulverston   121

Tour 8: The Coniston to Coniston Tour
Ambleside-Coniston-Skelwith Bridge-Red Bank-
Grasmere-Rydal-Ambleside   125

Tour 9: The Tarn Hows Tour
Ambleside-Tarn Hows-Coniston-Elter Water-
Clappersgate-Ambleside   128

Tour 10: Round the Langdales and Dungeon Ghyll Tour
Ambleside-Elter Water-Blea Tarn-Dungeon Ghyll-
Great Langdale-Red Bank-Grasmere-Rydal-Ambleside   131

Tour 11: The Ullswater Tour
Ambleside-Kirkstone Pass-Patterdale-Ullswater-
Patterdale-Troutbeck-Ambleside   135

Tour 14: The Wast Water Tour
Broughton-Seascale-Wast Water-Great Gable-
Wast Water-Seascale-Broughton   138

Tour 15: The Six Lakes Circular Tour
Ulverston-Haverthwaite-Ambleside-Thirlmere-
Keswick-Pooley Bridge-Ullswater-Patterdale-
Kirkstone Pass-Ambleside-Lakeside-Haverthwaite-
Ulverston   143

Tour 16: The Duddon Valley Tour
Ulverston-Foxfield-Broughton-Duddon Bridge-
Kirkhouse-Dunnerdale Hall-Newfield-Kirkhouse-Duddon
Bridge-Broughton-Foxfield-Ulverston   149

Tour 17: The Three Valleys Tour
Seascale-Gosforth-Santon Bridge-Irton Road-
Eskdale Green-Boot-Holmrook-Seascale   154

Index   158

An extract from an 1896 Furness Railway Map

Bibliography

Allen, Bob *Short Walks in the Lake District* (Michael Joseph Ltd, 1994)

Allen, Bob and Linney, Peter *Walking More Ridges of Lakeland* (Michael Joseph Ltd, 1996)

Andrews, Michael *The Furness Railway in and around Barrow* (Cumbrian Railways Association, 2003)

Andrews, Michael and Holne, Geoff *The Coniston Railway* (Cumbrian Railways Association, 2005)

Bradshaw, George *Bradshaw's Handbook for Tourists in Great Britain and Ireland* (first published 1866; online reprint, the Hathi Trust)

Cross, Derek *London Midland Steam in the Northern Fells* (D. Bradford Barton Ltd, 1974)

Davey, C. R. *Reflections of the Furness Railway* (Lakeland Heritage Books, 1984)

Davies, W. J. K *The Ravenglass & Eskdale Railway* (David & Charles, 1981)

Furness Railway *The Illustrated Guide to the Holiday Resorts on the Furness Railway* (Good Companion Books [reprint], 2007)

Hall, Victor *Industrial Steam Locomotives* (Bracken Books, 1977)

Heavyside, Tom *Lancashire & Cumberland's Last Days of Colliery Steam* (Stenlake, 2007)

Joy, David *A Regional History of the Railways of Great Britain*, Vol 14 *The Lake Counties* (David St John Thomas, 1983)

Linton, John *A Handbook of the Whitehaven and Furness Railway: being a Guide to the Lake District of West Cumberland and Furness* (R. Gibson & Son et al, 1852)

Robinson, Peter W. *Cumbria's Lost Railways* (Stenlake, 2002) *Railways of Cumbria* (Dalesman, 1980)

Rush, R. W. *The Furness Railway* (Oakwood Press, 1973)

Suggitt, Gordon *Lost Railways of Cumbria* (Countryside Books, 2008)

Various authors *Lancashire and Cumbria by Rail* (Jarrold & Sons, 1987)

Wainwright, Alfred *A Pictorial Guide to the Lakeland Fells* (Frances Lincoln [reprints], 2009)
Book 4 *The Southern Fells*
Book 5 *The Northern Fells*
Book 7 *The Western Fells*

Western, Robert *The Cockermouth, Keswick & Penrith Railway* (Oakwood Press, 2007)

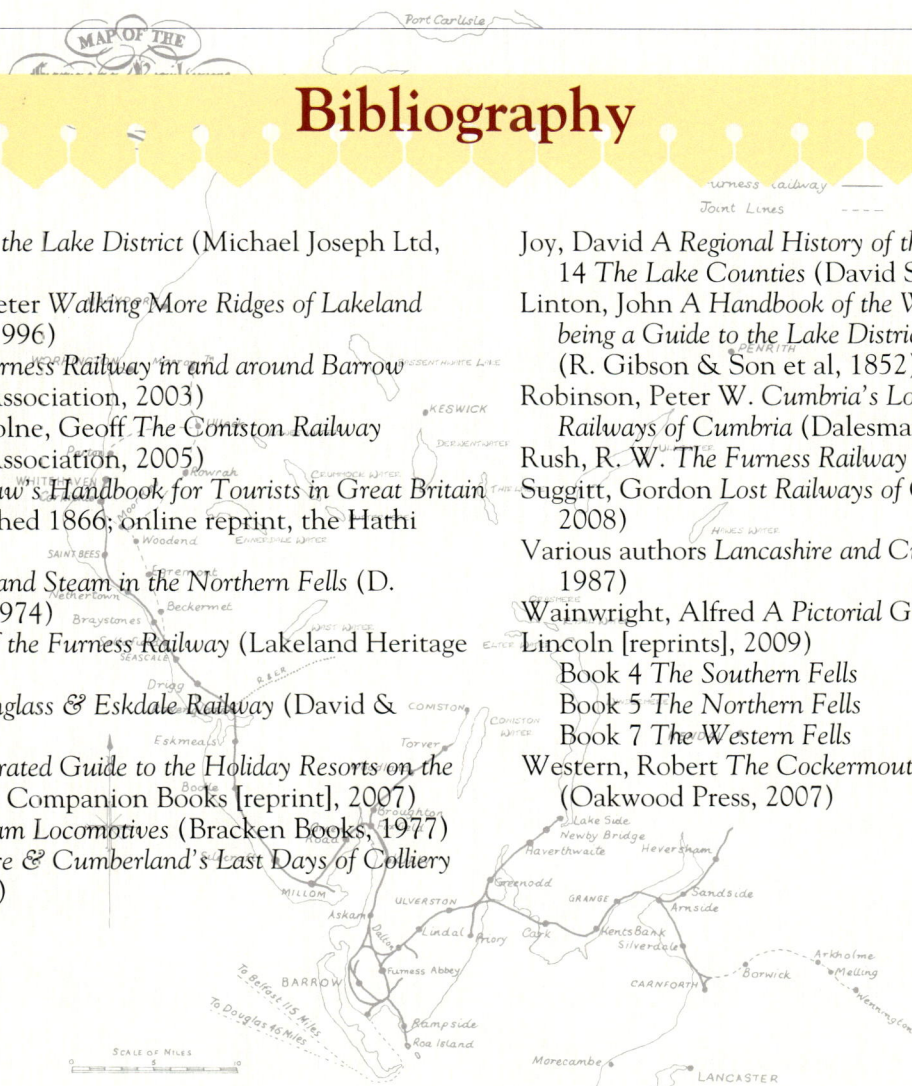

An extract from an 1896 Furness Railway Map

Preface

Background

Furness – the furthest 'ness,' or promontory – was one of the most remote parts of Britain. In the 1700s, when the fastest way to travel long distances was by stagecoach, it could take more than four days to journey from London to Carlisle. The arrival of the railways changed this and made the region accessible to all.

The first section of the Furness Railway (FR) was opened for traffic in 1846 following an unopposed passage of its Bill through Parliament, no doubt helped by its aristocratic origins. Although it started life as a mineral-carrying line, it quickly became notable for the facilities it offered to tourists wanting to explore the beautiful English Lake District. The company established itself as complete master of the area it served, which included some of the loveliest country in Britain, transporting vast quantities of mineral wealth to Barrow-in-Furness, which later became its headquarters. This hamlet with a few

farms and a population of less than 100 was to grow to a seething steel town of 60,000 in less than 40 years as a direct consequence of the bold development policies pursued by the management of the railway company. Barrow quickly became established as a railway centre with no fewer than ten stations within its boundaries. Unfortunately Barrow Central station, opened in 1882, was all but destroyed in air raids in 1941, yet by 1959 the rebuilding had been completed and the new station was renamed Barrow-in-Furness.

The boom time that transformed Barrow village began in the 1860s, following the rapid expansion of the Furness Railway's lines and the opening of Henry Schneider's huge Hindpool Steel Works, with its great blast furnaces. The Secretary and Superintendent of the FR, James Ramsden, was then able to put into operation his plan for the new Barrow, a model industrial town and port. Cooperation with the Midland Railway (MR) led to the moving of the Midland's steamer services from Morecambe to Barrow's Piel Pier to form the Barrow Steam Navigation Company. Its passenger

and freight services to Belfast and the Isle of Man were made profitable by means of the new partner's rail connections from Yorkshire and London. New and improved dock facilities soon followed with the building of Ramsden Dock in the 1870s, complete with a deep-water berth, and at the same time the railway empire of the FR continued to expand and thrive.

However, the FR's strained relationship with the MR came to a head in 1893, when the latter gave notice of termination of the partnership following its decision to build Heysham Harbour. In addition to this, railway traffic was in decline due to the exhaustion of the local iron ore upon which the company's lines had been so dependent. If the Furness Railway was to have a future, it would depend on the operation of passenger train services in association with its steamer traffic, which now included popular excursion sailings, particularly those to Blackpool. The company had one more vital advantage in its struggle for survival in those difficult times. On its doorstep was the unexploited splendour of the English Lake District.

Beginnings

The prime mover in the early days was William, Earl of Burlington, later to become the 7th Earl of Devonshire. His enterprise and foresight was the inspiration behind the idea for two short lines linking Kirkby-in-Furness (on the southern shore of the Duddon Estuary) and Dalton-in-Furness with the little port of Piel. Among the Earl's considerable land and financial interests in the Furness district of Lancashire were extensive slate quarries in the hills around Kirkby. These, together with newly discovered haematite iron ore in the Dalton area, offered great potential for profit as both needed to be transported to the coast for export by sea. Like the Earl of Lonsdale to the north, the Earl of Burlington realised the crucial role of the railways in moving these materials, and thus became intimately involved in the creation of the Furness Railway Company.

The company was incorporated in 1844, the same year as the Midland Railway. Like the Midland, the Furness would keep its original title throughout its life as an independent company until the 'Grouping' of 1923 created the 'Big Four'. In this respect it was exceeded in age only by the Great Western and the Maryport & Carlisle railways.

The first section of line from Kirkby to Dalton, together with a connecting link from Goldmire Junction to the original terminus at Rampside, both about 6 miles (10km) long, was inspected by the Board of Trade on 3 August 1846, and opened for traffic on the 12th. No special opening ceremony is recorded, presumably because the railway was intended primarily as a mineral line, and the first load, 100 tons of slate for shipment to Ireland, made its descent the day after opening. On visiting the nearby Furness Abbey, William Wordsworth was so incensed to find the railway being constructed adjacent to the ruins that he penned a sonnet contrasting the desecration being committed by the company with the respectful attitude of the navvies. He wrote:

'Profane despoilers, stand ye not reproved, while thus these simple-hearted men are moved?'

In spite of such sentiments, in 1848 progress continued with an extension northwards from Kirkby to Broughton in Furness, from where the company could pick up the copper ore traffic from the mines near

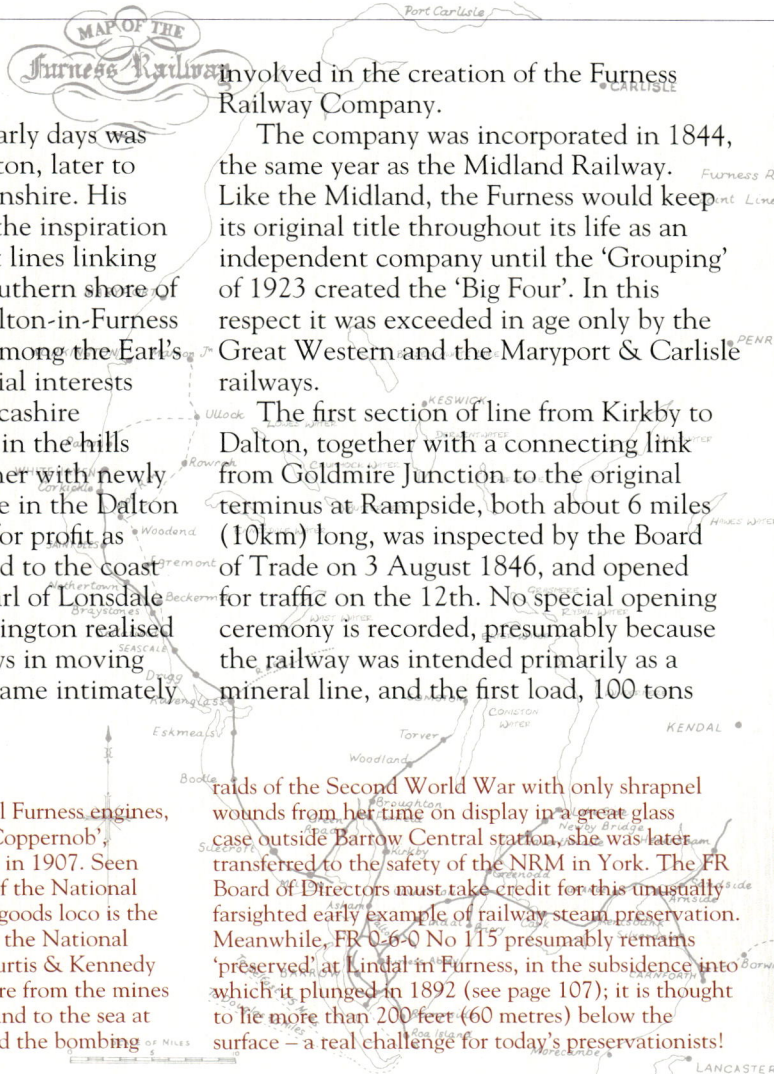

No 3, perhaps the best known of all Furness engines, and affectionately known as 'Old Coppernob', was introduced in 1846 and retired in 1907. Seen here on display in the Great Hall of the National Railway Museum, York, this 0-4-0 goods loco is the oldest loco with inside cylinders in the National Collection. It was built by Bury, Curtis & Kennedy of Liverpool in 1846 to haul iron ore from the mines of North Lancashire and Cumberland to the sea at Barrow-in-Furness. Having survived the bombing raids of the Second World War with only shrapnel wounds from her time on display in a great glass case outside Barrow Central station, she was later transferred to the safety of the NRM in York. The FR Board of Directors must take credit for this unusually farsighted early example of railway steam preservation. Meanwhile, FR 0-6-0 No 115 presumably remains 'preserved' at Lindal in Furness, in the subsidence into which it plunged in 1892 (see page 107); it is thought to lie more than 200 feet (60 metres) below the surface – a real challenge for today's preservationists!

An extract from an 1896 Furness Railway Map

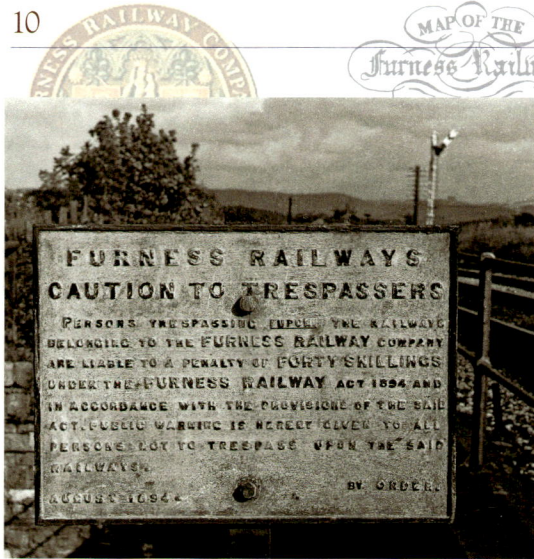

A Furness Railway cast-iron 'Caution to Trespassers' sign seen near Ulverston in 1974, warning of liability to 'a penalty of Forty Shillings' (£2) for the offence of trespassing on the company's railway. The sign is dated August 1894.

Coniston. The copper was first transported down the lake in large iron barges constructed by John Wilkinson, famed for having built the first iron bridge in England at Ironbridge in Shropshire. By this time the increased mineral traffic, together with the newly provided passenger trains, was placing huge demands on the company's six 'Bury' locomotives, which were finding it increasingly hard to cope.

By the early 1850s Ulverston was one of many towns regretting its earlier hostility to the coming of the railway, realising that its continued dependence on the treacherous 'over-sands' journey as the 'nearest and cheapest route to Lancaster' was outmoded. The town was finally connected by rail in 1854 after delays caused by the need for the construction of difficult cuttings, the then Ulverstone & Lancaster Railway Company's route continued eastwards past the Cavendish family seat at Holker Hall, through Grange-over-Sands to Arnside, to join the Lancaster & Carlisle Railway (L&CR) line to Carnforth. Thus the company's early weakness, that the line 'pointed in the wrong direction', i.e. north towards Whitehaven, was resolved and the need for a direct link to the expanding markets of Yorkshire, Lancashire, the Midlands and South Wales by way of the L&CR was achieved. The new railway shortened the dry land distance from Ulverston to Lancaster from 34 miles (54km) to less than 25 miles (40km). This, combined with the disaster 3 months prior to completion of the route when 12 young men had been drowned while attempting to cross the sands, was seen as heralding in a new era, hailed as 'a new and delightful route to the far-famed ruins of Furness Abbey and the Cumberland Lake District'.

The crest of the Furness Railway Company is derived from the seal of Furness Abbey, and incorporates symbols of Lord Cavendish, the Duke of Devonshire, a major shareholder.

The chain of railways stretching right round the Cumbrian coast was thus completed, opening the door for an economic revolution in the Furness region, the catalyst for which had been the discovery in 1850 of the massive haematite deposits in the Dalton area, alongside the Broughton line.

It was during this period that the company was taking steps to develop the little town of Barrow-in-Furness as a port. Screw steamers already operated from here to Fleetwood and other places across Morecambe Bay, and the potential for expansion was attractive. By 1855 things were going very well for the Furness Railway, with passenger traffic increasing and mineral carriage booming, bringing with it the need for track-doubling over considerable lengths of the railway. The establishment in 1859 of Messrs Schneider & Hannay steelworks at Barrow set the seal on the future prosperity of the Furness Railway Company. Later becoming the Barrow Haematite Steel Company, these extensive works and blast furnaces generated major traffic in pig iron and coke. Expansion of the Furness Railway continued, with three other companies being taken over within the next five years. The Ulverstone & Lancaster and the Coniston Railway companies became part of the growing 'empire' in 1862, with the Whitehaven & Furness Junction Railway being added in 1866. Shortly afterwards, plans to take over the rapidly developing harbour at Barrow came to fruition, as did a scheme for a new joint line with the 'Little North Western' from Carnforth to Wennington Junction on the Midland Railway. The idea was to obtain a through route to Yorkshire and the Midlands from where large amounts of traffic could be expected to flow to Barrow for export.

Also at this time a start had been made on a branch from Ulverston to Newby Bridge, leaving the main line at Plumpton Junction (about 1½ miles [2.5km] from Ulverston), with intermediate stations at Greenodd and Haverthwaite. Another mineral branch was opened from Crooklands to Stainton in 1868 to tap into a large limestone deposit that was to be worked to supply the local blast furnaces. In 1868 it was decided to extend the Newby Bridge branch up to the end of Windermere at Lakeside, cleverly anticipating the growth of the tourist traffic in this area to add to the important freight to and from the charcoal blast furnace at Backbarrow. Over the next ten years the company energetically developed its business and assets to consolidate the Furness Railway as the most important transport provider in the area. It remained so until 1923.

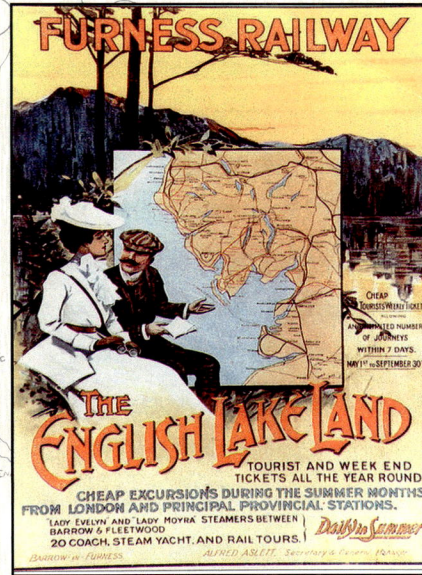

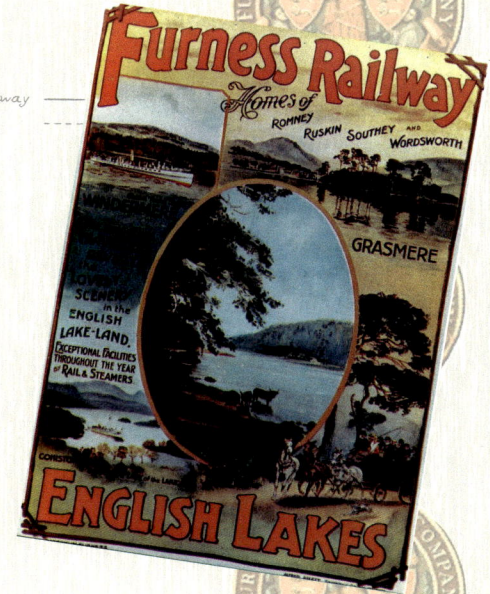

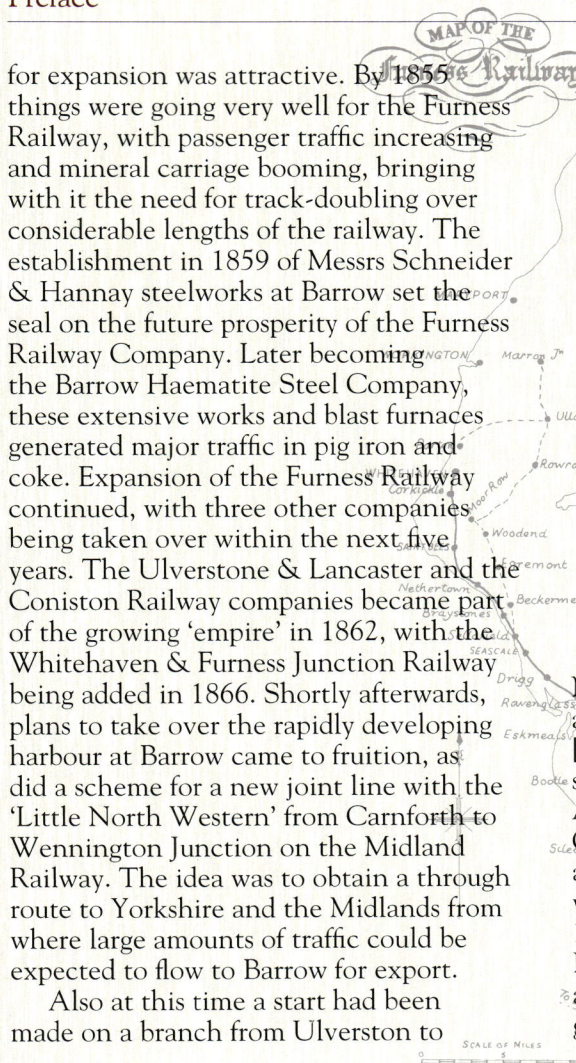

Furness Railway postcards: 'The English Lake Land' and 'English Lakes', both circa 1910.

Introduction: The Furness Railway Tours

By the end of the 19th century, it was increasingly felt that the Furness Railway Company was in something of a rut, with a passenger service some thought 'uninspired', coaching stock that was out of date and locomotive power that was inadequate to handle the increasing tourist and freight traffic. The leadership had served the company long and well, but it was becoming obvious that some 'new blood' might be needed to instil more vigour and enterprise into the administration. Such an event was to take place in 1895 with the appointment of Mr Alfred Aslett, first as Secretary and later also as General Manager. His appointment coincided with an upturn in the iron trade following a particularly difficult period for the Barrow Haematite Steel Company, one of the FR's most important customers.

This improvement in the company's circumstances allowed Aslett to concentrate on the things he did best. He was from the Cambrian Railways, which relied heavily on passenger traffic for its revenue. It was to this source that the company now looked

for increasing returns, and the new Manager wasted no time in putting a number of fresh plans into practice, quickly realising the potential of the company's territory from a tourism point of view and seeing clearly that too little attention had been paid to this source of potential revenue. He noticed that only four rail and coach tours were in operation in an area crying out for an integrated system to allow visitors to experience the stunning landscape. He immediately organised no fewer than 20, unashamedly aimed at the growing number of well-off Victorian 'tourists' with the time and the financial resources to 'broaden their horizons' by means of day-long excursions. To promote his venture, the company commissioned a series of colourful postcards showing the Lake District in all its glory and featuring the many places of interest that might be visited by patrons on the tours. To illustrate the tours, many of these are included in the following pages.

Although tourist bookings had been introduced as early as 1859, when the *Gondola* first sailed on Coniston Water, the extension of the FR to Lakeside

on Windermere in 1869 presented the opportunity to introduce 'Circular Tours' – a prospect eagerly recognised by Henry Cook, the company's Traffic manager. Gaps in the routes between railway and steamer stations were covered by horse-drawn omnibuses (carriages) running between such places as Ambleside and Coniston, Coniston Lake Bank and Greenodd, and between Windermere town and Bowness. Henry Cook's early tours were soon increased to the 20 established under Aslett's leadership, which continued successfully until the First World War halted them for a time, after which they were resumed and continued into LMS days.

The pride of Mr Aslett's heart was his 'Six Lakes Tour', which embraced Windermere, Ullswater, Derwent Water, Thirlmere, Grasmere and Rydal Water, all for the 'bargain price' of 'from 12 shillings' – this at a time when the average full-time working wage was about £1 (20 shillings) per week. It included steamer fares on Windermere and Ullswater, coach travel between these two lakes, the journey

FURNESS RAILWAY.
The Gateway to the ENGLISH LAKES.

20
Rail, Coach, and Steam Yacht Tours through Lake-Land,
IN OPERATION EVERY WEEK-DAY, FROM
Whitsuntide to End of September.
EMBRACING:—
Windermere, Rydal, Coniston, Grasmere, Thirlmere, Derwentwater, Ullswater, Wastwater, Ennerdale, &c., Lakes, Furness Abbey, and George Romney's Home (1742 to 1755).

Blackpool and the Lakes
via FLEETWOOD & BARROW
BY THE
P.S. "LADY EVELYN" or "LADY MOYRA."
DAILY SAILINGS (INCLUDING SUNDAYS),
From Whitsuntide to End of September.
GRAND CIRCULAR TOURS.

TOURISTS' WEEKLY TICKETS
Between certain groups of Stations, available for an unlimited number of Journeys.
ALFRED ASLETT,
Barrow-in-Furness, March, 1914.   Secretary & General Manager.

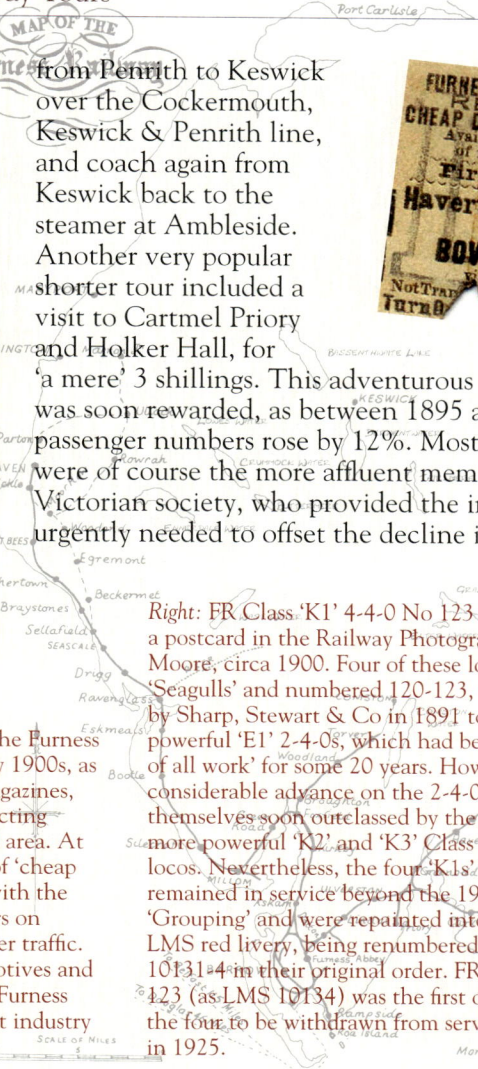

from Penrith to Keswick over the Cockermouth, Keswick & Penrith line, and coach again from Keswick back to the steamer at Ambleside. Another very popular shorter tour included a visit to Cartmel Priory and Holker Hall, for 'a mere' 3 shillings. This adventurous policy was soon rewarded, as between 1895 and 1898 passenger numbers rose by 12%. Most of these were of course the more affluent members of Victorian society, who provided the income urgently needed to offset the decline in other

revenues caused by the trade slump during this period; for example, in 1896 the Barrow steelworks closed for six months with 6,000 men being put out of work.

As well as the tours, another of Aslett's success stories was the reopening of the Barrow-Fleetwood steamer service, which had been withdrawn in 1870. By 1899 circumstances had changed dramatically with the rise of Blackpool as a thriving holiday resort, raising the prospect of two-way traffic from Blackpool via Fleetwood and Barrow for the tours, and from Barrow

Above and above right: Advertisements for the Furness Railway's tours appeared widely in the early 1900s, as posters at railway stations, in books and magazines, and in the form of the many postcards depicting the undeniable attraction of this wonderful area. At the same time the introduction of a series of 'cheap day' and cheaper weekly tickets, together with the introduction of a Sunday service of steamers on Windermere, considerably boosted passenger traffic. The acquisition of bigger and better locomotives and improved coaching stock consolidated the Furness Railway's position at the heart of the tourist industry in the Lake District.

Right: FR Class 'K1' 4-4-0 No 123 is portrayed on a postcard in the Railway Photographs Series by F. Moore, circa 1900. Four of these locos, nicknamed 'Seagulls' and numbered 120-123, were supplied by Sharp, Stewart & Co in 1891 to replace the less powerful 'E1' 2-4-0s, which had been the FR 'maids of all work' for some 20 years. However, though a considerable advance on the 2-4-0s, the 'K1s' were themselves soon outclassed by the still more powerful 'K2' and 'K3' Class locos. Nevertheless, the four 'K1s' remained in service beyond the 1923 'Grouping' and were repainted into LMS red livery, being renumbered 10131-4 in their original order. FR No 123 (as LMS 10134) was the first of the four to be withdrawn from service, in 1925.

An extract from an 1896 Furness Railway Map

and the Furness district to Fleetwood and Blackpool. Consequently in August 1900 the *Lady Evelyn* arrived in Barrow and the service to Fleetwood was operational once more. So successful was she that in 1904 she was lengthened by 30 feet (9 metres) to increase her passenger accommodation. She remained in service with the company until requisitioned by the Admiralty in 1914. The *Lady Margaret* was added in 1903, to be replaced by *Philomel* in 1908, which in turn was replaced by *Lady Moyra* in 1910. By the end of the 1912 season, Aslett had increased passenger bookings on the FR by 53% and passenger revenue by

44%. While all this was happening Aslett had also successfully reduced operating expenses to make the company's ratio of expenses to receipts the lowest of all the country's railways. To further add to the attraction, it was during this time that the touring motor charabanc was gaining

in popularity. In spite of the noise and eccentricity of early engines, people took to the charabanc enthusiastically so that by 1914, in the form of an enormous open touring car on solid tyres, it was rapidly becoming the preferred option by which to explore the succession of beauty spots encountered on the tours.

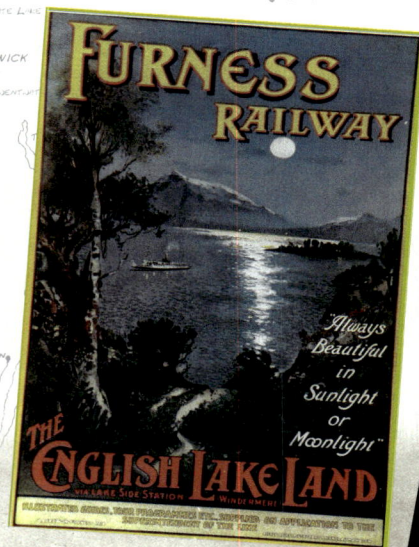

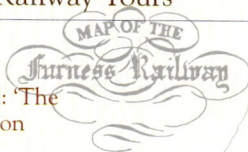

Opposite top left to right: FR postcard: 'The English Lakeland via Lakeside Station (Windermere)', circa 1904.

FR postcard: 'The English Lake Land', circa 1910.

FR postcard: 'All Roads lead to Lake-Land', circa 1905.

Opposite bottom: 'K2' Class 4-4-0 No 32 (renumbered from 21) was built by Sharp, Stewart & Co in 1896, and is seen here on a post card by Raphael Tuck & Sons Ltd for the Furness Railway ('FR Rolling Stock [The Present]', Series No 19, circa 1900. Fitted with 6-foot coupled driving wheels, the largest hitherto seen on the line, she became LMS No 10137 and remained in service until 1930.

Right: Proudly displayed in steam at 'Railfest 2012' at the National Railway Museum, York, is the Furness Railway Trust's flagship loco, 0-4-0 No 20, one of eight such tender locos supplied to the company between 1863 and 1866. No 20 is the oldest working standard-gauge steam locomotive in the UK, having been built for the FR by Sharp, Stewart & Co of Manchester in 1863, to haul iron ore and slate trains to Barrow-in-Furness. She was preserved and restored to full working order by the Furness Railway Trust in 1999.

The Furness Railway Illustrated Guides

The Illustrated Guides published by the company in the early years of the 20th century gave details of the '20 Coach and Steam Yacht Tours Through Lakeland' that were offered every weekday from June to September.

These excellent and invaluable Guides also gave descriptions of all the major towns and large villages along the railway, as well as listing details of hotels and farmhouse, country and seaside lodgings in the area. 'The English Lake-Land', a guide issued

Furness Railway Tours for the 1905 season

Tour 1: The Outer Circular Tour, embracing Windermere, Furness Abbey and Coniston. Fare from 5/3d

Tour 2: The Inner Circular Tour, embracing Furness Abbey, Coniston Lake (by Steam Yacht 'Gondola') and the Crake Valley. Fare from 3/3d

Tour 3: The Grange and Windermere Circular Tour, embracing Grange, Kendal and Windermere Lake. Fare from 2/9d

Tour 4: The Middle Circular Tour, embracing Windermere Lake, the Crake Valley and Coniston Lake. Fare from 5/9d

Tour 5: The Red Bank and Grasmere Tour, via Ambleside and Skelwith Force. Fare from 2/9d

Tour 6: The Thirlmere, Grasmere and Windermere Tour, via Ambleside, Clappersgate and Red Bank. Fare from 5/-

Tour 7: The Four Lakes Circular Tour, viz Coniston, Grasmere, Rydal and Windermere. Fare from 5/9d

Tour 8: The Coniston to Coniston Tour, via Red Bank, Grasmere and Ambleside. Fare from 4/6d

Tour 9: The Tarn Hows Tour, via Ambleside and Coniston, returning via Tilberthwaite and Elterwater. Fare from 4/6d

Tour 10: The Round the Langdales and Dungeon Ghyll Tour, via Ambleside, Colwith Force, Grasmere and Rydal. Fare from 5/-

Tour 11: The Ullswater Tour, via Ambleside, Kirkstone Pass and Brothers Water, returning via the Vale of Troutbeck and Low Wood. Fare from 5/6d

Tour 12: The Derwentwater (Keswick) Tour, via Ambleside, Grasmere and Thirlmere. Fare from 6/-

Tour 13: The Five Lakes Circular Tour, viz Windermere, Rydal, Grasmere, Thirlmere and Derwentwater. Fare from 11/6d

Tour 14: The Wastwater Tour, via Seascale and Gosforth. Fare from 4/6d

Tour 15: The Six Lakes Circular Tour, viz Windermere, Rydal, Grasmere, Thirlmere, Derwentwater and Ullswater. Fare from 12/-

Tour 16: The Duddon Valley Tour, via Broughton in Furness, Ulpha and Seathwaite. Fare from 3/9d

Tour 17: The Three Valleys Tour, via the Irt, Esk & Mite, via Seascale, Gosforth and Boot, returning via Holmrook

Tour 18: The Ennerdale Lake and Calder Abbey Tour, via Seascale, Gosforth and Cold Fell. Fare from 4/6d

Tour 19: The 'Across the Ferry' Tour, via Esthwaite Water, Hawkshead, Ferry and Storrs Hall. Fare from 3/6d

Tour 20: The Cartmel Priory and Newby Bridge Tour, via Windermere (Lakeside), Holker Park and Grange. Fare from 3/-

Also advertised in the 1905 Guide were 'Grand Evening Cruises between Fleetwood and Barrow' by the PS *Lady Margaret*, a 3-hour sailing every evening during the summer season; the fare was 1 shilling, with a band and refreshments on board. 'Sundays at Blackpool' operated every Sunday evening during the season between Barrow and Fleetwood (for Blackpool) by the PS *Lady Evelyn*.

An extract from an 1896 Furness Railway Map

MAP OF THE
Furness Railway
AND CONNECTIONS

SCALE OF MILES

P.S. LADY MOYRA.

FURNESS RAILWAY.
STEAMER SERVICE
BETWEEN
BARROW & FLEETWOOD
(for Blackpool)
and CONISTON LAKE
SUSPENDED FOR
1915 SEASON

Furness Railway and
connections shewn thus
Steamer Routes
Coach Tours

Refreshment Rooms
at Stations, &c.,
underlined : Ulverston

Other Railways

Golf at Stations marked

by the Furness Railway in 1911, advertises a 'Splendid Service of Steam Yachts on Windermere and Coniston Lakes, running in connection with trains and coaches.' In its introduction to the English Lake District, it notes that it was described by Wordsworth as 'The loveliest spot that Man hath ever found', and that

'...it is a district of beautiful lakes, of wooded slopes, of waterfalls and glens and of mountains of infinite variety and form. Its unexcelled natural beauty has attracted some of the greatest of English Litterateurs; it was the chosen home of Wordsworth, Southey, Ruskin, the Coleridges, Shelley, Mrs Hemans, Harriett Martineau and many more of our foremost lovers of the beautiful in nature.'

Another FR Illustrated Guide issued during the First World War in 1916, entitled 'The English Lakeland, Paradise of Tourists', while lamenting the suspension 'until further notice' of its steamers to Fleetwood, Blackpool and the Isle of Man, together with a number of the Lakeland Tours, nevertheless continued to cordially encourage visitors to the area. The issue opened its description of the English Lakeland as a holiday resort with this glowing accolade:

'It may be said with all truth, that no Railway in England possesses more natural and acquired attractions for the tourist and holiday maker than the Furness Railway. Its chief is that it is the line which traverses the Southern and South Western portion of the famous English Lake District – that wonderful area possessing literary associations which are forever immortal, and a wealth of scenery without equal anywhere else in the world.'

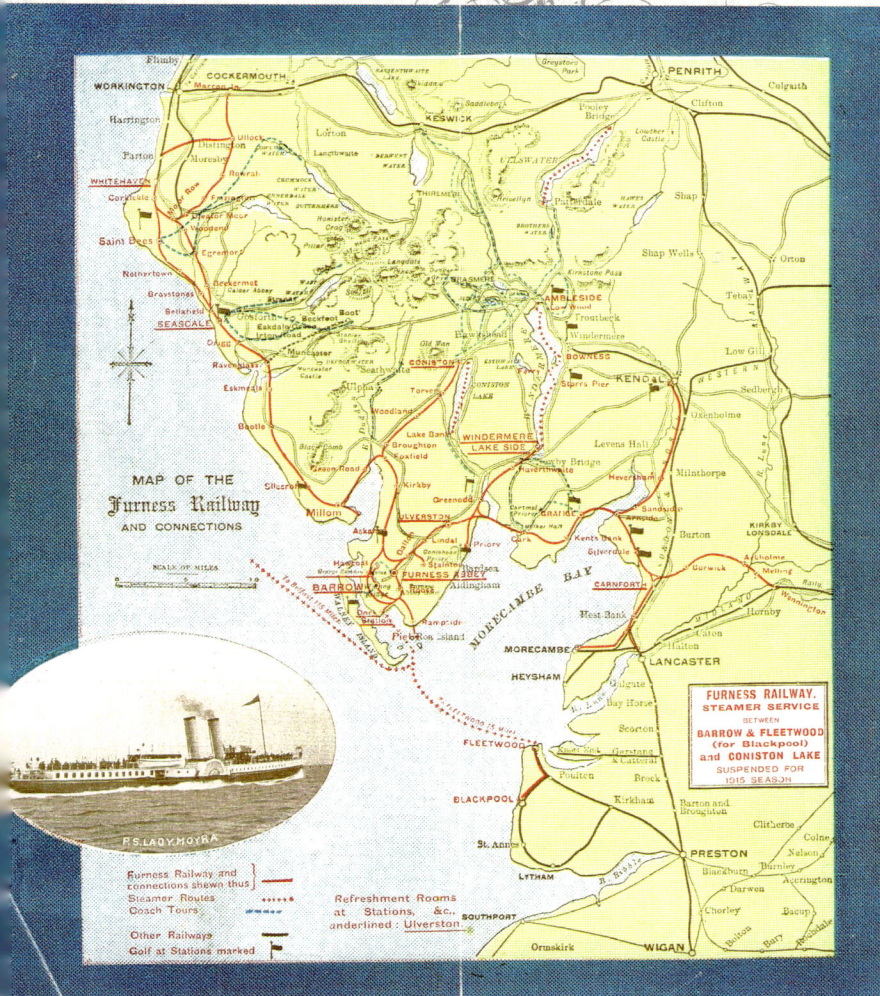

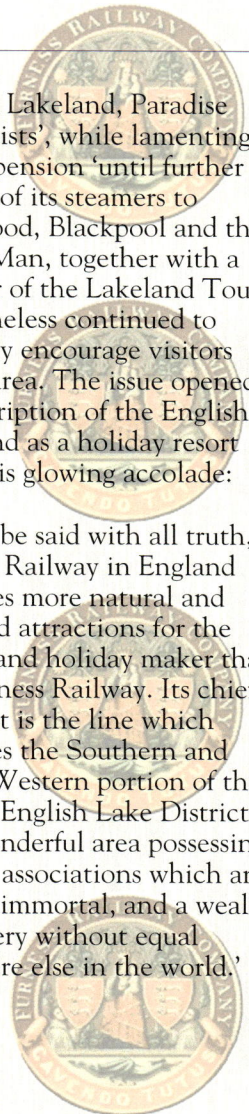

An extract from an 1896 Furness Railway Map

Sources of information

For the latest travel and tourism information, please refer to the appropriate publications available from Tourist Information Centres (TICs) and other outlets located in most towns, which provide information on what to see and do, including events, entertainment, places of interest, travel, transport and where to stay. A full list of TICs for Cumbria and the Lake District can be found at www.visitcumbria.com/touristin-formation-centres.

Alternatively, visit websites such as: www.golakes.co.uk (for local attractions and information)
www.firstnorthwestern.co.uk (for local train times and services)
www.cumbria.gov.uk/buses (for bus timetables and services)
www.cumbriawildlifetrust.org.uk (for local nature reserves)
www.windermere-lakecruises.co.uk
www.ullswater-steamers.co.uk
www.keswick-launch.co.uk
www.conistonlaunch.co.uk
www.lakesiderailway.co.uk
www.ravenglass-railway.co.uk
www.barrowtourism.co.uk

Cumbria County Council publishes a free and very useful Bus Timetable and Travel Guide entitled 'Go Cumbria', containing timetables for the main bus services throughout the county together with town service maps, a guide to the rail network and ferry service details. The guide can be downloaded from www.cumbria.gov.uk/landing_page/roadsandtravel.asp, or you can pick up a copy from any TIC or library in the region.

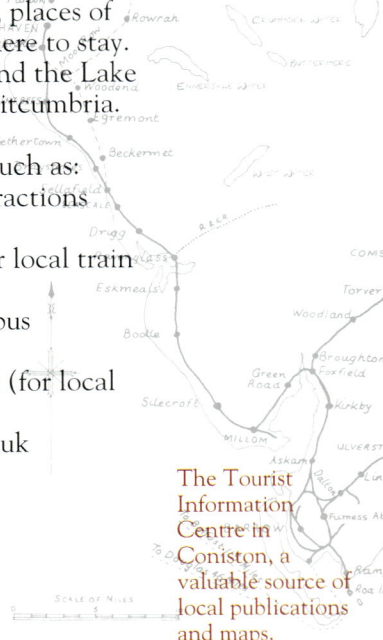

The Tourist Information Centre in Coniston, a valuable source of local publications and maps.

An extract from an 1896 Furness Railway Map

Note: 'Day Ranger' tickets are available for travel over some of these routes. Some tickets also cover Stagecoach bus and Windermere Lake Steamer services in addition to rail services throughout the region. For details and prices please visit www. northernrail.org, and click on 'Tickets', 'Rangers and Rovers', then 'Explore Cumbria and the Lake District'.

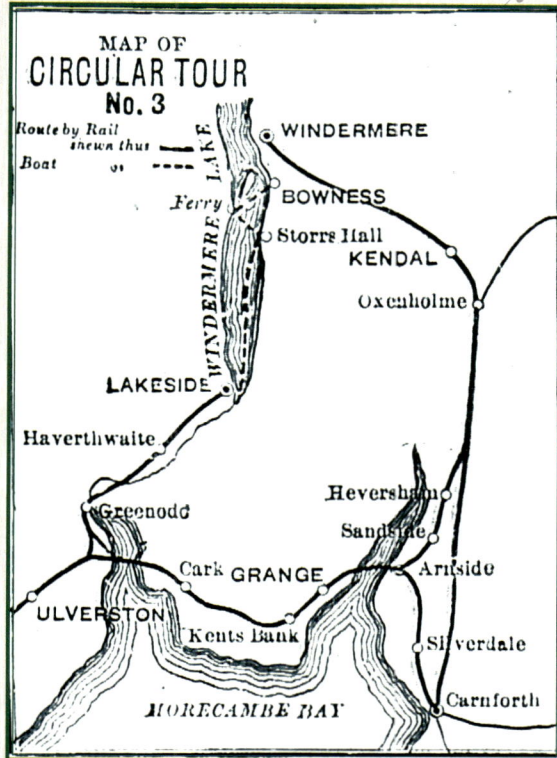

MAP OF
CIRCULAR TOUR
No. 3

Route by Rail
shewn thus
Boat

Tour 3: The Grange and Windermere Circular Tour
Carnforth-Arnside-Ulverston-Greenodd-Haverthwaite-Lakeside-Bowness-Windermere-Kendal-Oxenholme-Carnforth

By national rail from Carnforth to Ulverston – bus to Haverthwaite – heritage railway to Lakeside – boat to Bowness – national rail from Windermere to Carnforth via Oxenholme and Lancaster

- Allow about 6½ hours for the full itinerary (can be shortened)
- Suggested starting point: Carnforth railway station

The Furness line departs from the West Coast Main Line at Carnforth, one-time home of the Steamtown Railway Museum, now operated by the rail-tour operator West Coast Railway Company. The route through Barrow-in-Furness and along the western fringe of the Lake District, through Whitehaven and Workington to Carlisle, is today known as the Cumbrian Coast Line.

Carnforth station, north of Lancaster, was opened in 1846 by the Lancaster & Carlisle Railway, and originally had just a single platform. Following its connection with the lines of the Furness and Midland companies in 1856, it was progressively enlarged and eventually completely rebuilt in 1880. A further rebuild by the LMS in 1937 included a platform 890 feet (about 270 metres) long to accommodate the Furness line trains, as Carnforth developed into a bustling railway junction linking stations across the North West of England from Cumberland to Leeds.

Following the end of steam traction and the reorganisation of Britain's railways

An extract from an 1896 Furness Railway Map

Tour 3: Typical journey times

By rail
dep Carnforth 09.08 to Ulverston (approx 35 mins)
By bus (X6)
dep Ulverston 09.52 to Haverthwaite (approx 15 mins)
By rail (L&HR)
dep Haverthwaite 10.35 to Lakeside (approx 20 mins)
By boat
dep Lakeside 11.20 to Bowness (approx 30 mins)
Lunch in Bowness
By bus (599)
dep Bowness 13.30 to Windermere (approx 10 mins)
By rail
dep Windermere 14.00 to Lancaster (changing at Oxenholme) (approx 40 mins)
By rail
dep Lancaster 15.34 to Carnforth (approx 10 mins)
or
By bus (55 or 555)
dep Lancaster Bus Station (10 mins walk from railway station) 14.50 to Carnforth Haws Hill (approx 25 mins, plus 10 mins walking time back to Carnforth railway station)

Note: Bus, rail and ferry timetables can change at very short notice. Be sure to check details before travelling.

following the Beeching Report in the 1960s, the station was gradually run down; the main-line platforms were removed in 1970, and it was reduced to the status of a branch-line facility. As a result no West Coast Main Line express services now call at the town. However, following a major restoration project the station buildings have been reopened as the Carnforth Station Heritage and Visitor Centre, boasting the 'Brief Encounter Refreshment Rooms', inspired by the David Lean romantic classic filmed here in 1945 starring Celia Johnson and Trevor Howard.

The station has a car park with 64 spaces and sheltered cycle storage on the platform. The ticket office is open daily from 06.30 to 18.10

CARNFORTH Stanier 'Black 5' 4-6-0 No 44709 is seen at Carnforth shed, coded 11A, on 8 August 1968, just three days before BR's date for the end of steam on the network. Built in 1948 at Horwich Locomotive Works, No 44709 was still to be seen working on the West Coast Main Line and into Barrow-in-Furness until withdrawal later that month; it was subsequently cut up at Draper's Neptune Street scrapyard in Hull on 30 November. A total of 578 steam locos were disposed of through Draper's yard, including many more 'Black 5s', 'Jubilees', 'Royal Scots', Gresley 'A3s', Peppercorn 'A1s', Thompson 'B1s', 'WD' 8Fs and Riddles BR 9F 2-10-0s.

CARNFORTH 'Black 5' No 44962 races through Carnforth station in 1960.

Monday to Friday and 07.30 to 15.30 on Saturday, but closed on Sunday. Trains run at approximately hourly intervals. There is no service over the Cumbrian Coast Line on Sundays. First TransPennine Express and Northern Rail run trains from Carnforth to Barrow-in-Furness, operating a regular service calling at Silverdale (most trains), Arnside, Grange-over-Sands and Ulverston. The journey to Ulverston takes about 35 minutes.

Silverdale is a pleasant village, set in an attractive and unspoilt area popular with visitors in the summer; the sea is a pleasant 20-minute walk from the station, along a quiet road and footpath. The village boasts a handsome 'new' church built in 1886 and a rather plain 'old' church erected in 1829. Just outside the station is the Leighton Moss nature reserve, managed by the Royal Society for the Protection of Birds (www.rspb.org.uk), containing the largest area of reed-beds in North West England, together with lagoons and woodlands, forming a wetland of international importance on the edge of Morecambe Bay.

Walks centred on the village are of great interest, with the Pepper Pot (on Castlebarrow Head), the Cove with its caves, Jenny Brown's Point and the wells at Woodwell and Burton Well all inviting exploration. The station itself boasts a restaurant converted from the old station house.

About 2 miles (3.2km) further on we arrive at the small seaside town of **Arnside** with its promenade and embankment along the Kent Estuary, constructed in 1897, and the impressive 51-span viaduct over the River Kent where it meets Morecambe Bay. Constructed in 1856, the Grade II listed structure was closed to traffic for a 16-week period in 2011 while the entire deck was completely rebuilt. Close to the promenade is an inn named Ye Olde Fighting Cocks, which dates from 1660.

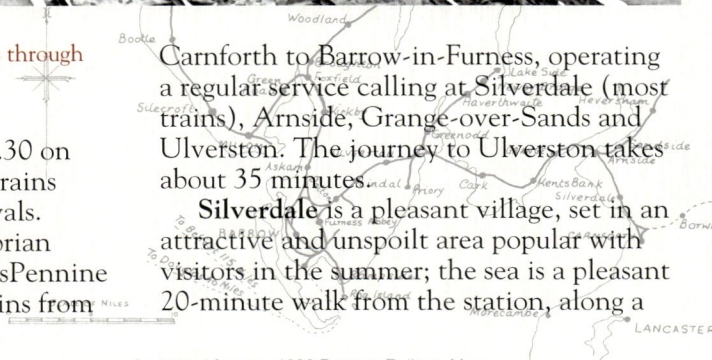

An extract from an 1896 Furness Railway Map

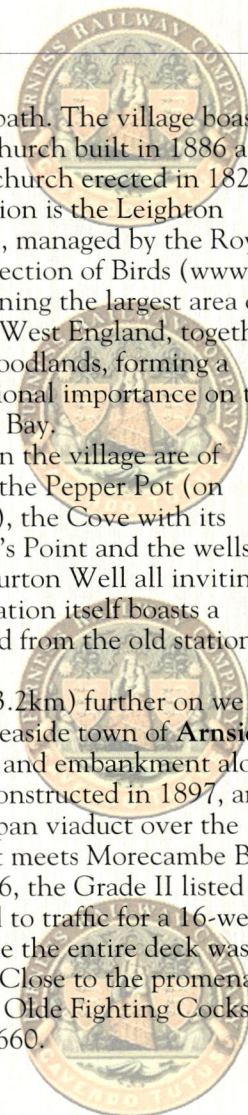

Above the station, the fine headland of Arnside Knott (522 feet [160 metres]) affords stunning views across Morecambe Bay and, beyond the viaduct, to Whitbarrow and the southern Lakeland Fells. This northern part of Morecambe Bay constitutes the Arnside and Silverdale Area of Outstanding Natural Beauty (www.arnsidesilverdaleaonb.org.uk), and within it are the nature reserves of Gait Barrows and Warton Crag; both are worth a visit by

Left: **ARNSIDE** and the viaduct are viewed from Arnside Knott, as a Barrow-in-Furness to Manchester Airport service crosses the bay.

Below left: **ARNSIDE** Crossing the viaduct before passing through the station at Arnside on 15 May 2014 is a train carrying low-level radioactive waste from Sellafield, heading for Crewe and hauled by double-headed DRS Class 37s Nos 37608 and 37607.

Below: **ARNSIDE PIER** is an example of the changes brought about by the coming of the railway. A plaque beside the pier tells the story: 'Following an Act of Parliament, the pier was constructed by the Ulverston and Lancaster Railway Co, replacing an earlier wooden structure. It was built to provide a wharf for sea-borne traffic after the construction of the viaduct across the estuary had prevented ships from reaching the port of Milnthorpe. The end section of the pier was destroyed by storm in 1934 and was rebuilt by the London Midland and Scottish Railway Co.'

GAIT BARROWS NATURE RESERVE Specialities of the nature reserve include the Duke of Burgundy fritillary and the Lady's Slipper orchid.

WARTON CRAG NATURE RESERVE A peregrine falcon patrols the rock face.

those interested in the animals and plants associated with this very special habitat.

The arrival of the new railway was not greeted as good news by everyone, as is documented in what is now the Albion Hotel in Arnside. Originally a private house owned by Captain Robert Greenwood, an important player in the local fishing industry, the railway sounded the death knell for coastal trading in the Kent Estuary. The Captain's daughter Isabella married Richard Bush, a partner in her father's maritime business, and after the Captain's death Richard wisely anticipated the future

and altered the family house, opening it as 'Bush's Albion Hotel'. Bars and function rooms were provided for the anticipated increase in custom brought by the railway, together with a coach and carriage service to cater for the needs of the expected wealthy visitors. Such was the success of his venture that the Albion Hotel survives and prospers to this day, welcoming visitors to Arnside by whatever means they arrive.

Full details of the walks around Silverdale and Arnside can be obtained locally.

Just beyond Arnside a diverging branch

line headed north-east through Sandside and Heversham to join the London & North Western Railway (LNWR) main line at Hincaster Junction, south of Oxenholme, before going on through Kendal to Windermere. The branch was constructed as a result of an agreement with the LNWR, signed in 1865, that the latter would not build any more lines west of its Lancaster & Carlisle main line. Instead, the new line, known as the Furness & Lancaster & Carlisle Union Railway, would be of benefit to both companies in that the Furness

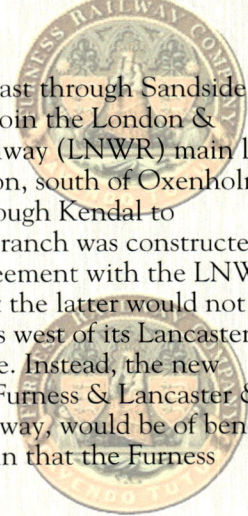

An extract from an 1896 Furness Railway Map

would receive a direct route for its coke and iron ore trains from the North Eastern Railway via Tebay, while the LNWR would gain revenue from the traffic passing over its section from Hincaster Junction to Tebay. The branch was closed to passenger trains in 1942 and the track north of Sandside was lifted in 1963. When freight traffic from Sandside Quarry ended in 1971 the remainder of the line closed, although

sections of the trackbed can still be made out, for example along the Kent Estuary at Sandside.

After crossing the lengthy Kent Viaduct we stay close to Morecambe Bay as we head for **Grange-over-Sands**. The viaduct provided the first easy access to the coast north of Morecambe Bay and enabled Grange-over-Sands to develop to become a major Victorian resort created largely by

the Furness Railway. The delightful town with its fine 19th-century architecture enjoys a position sheltered by the hills from the cold north and north-easterly winds, producing a milder climate that encouraged its growth as a favourite health resort. Today Grange is an ideal base from which to explore the area, perhaps including the nearby Hampsfell Nature Trail, or further afield by local bus from the railway station to places such as Cartmel for the famous Priory, or Haverthwaite for the steam railway. The railway station, a Grade II listed building restored in 1997/98, is adjacent to the promenade that runs along the edge of Morecambe Bay, providing excellent views across the estuary. Next to the station are the well-maintained Ornamental Gardens, enclosing a lake inhabited by a variety of water birds.

Beyond Grange the

Nr SANDSIDE Part of the trackbed of the branch line from Arnside to Hincaster Junction, near Oxenholme on the LNWR, is now a pleasant footpath along the River Kent estuary near Sandside.

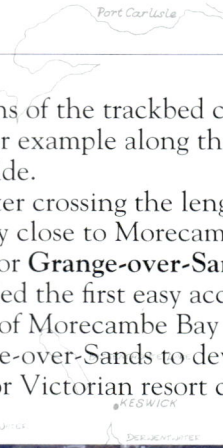

Right: **GRANGE-OVER-SANDS** 'Black 5' No 44932 heads 'The Lakelander' steam railtour towards Grange-over-Sands on 17 July 2010, with the River Kent estuary and Morecambe Bay in the background.

Below: **GRANGE-OVER-SANDS** A Furness Railway postcard showing Grange-over-Sands in about 1910. Like many such postcards published by the company, the name of the nearest FR station was included for the benefit of the traveller.

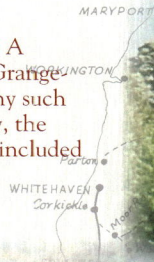

GRANGE-OVER-SANDS.
GRANGE STATION.

An extract from an 1896 Furness Railway Map

railway passes through Kents Bank and Cark as it continues to skirt Morecambe Bay on its way to our next destination, the historic market town of Ulverston. **Kents Bank** is famous for its dangerous crossing over the sands to Hest Bank, a distance of 8 miles (13km). Before the railway offered a fast and safe means of travel, many preferred this hazardous journey to the alternative, a road journey of 30 miles (48km).

For a time, after the dissolution of Furness Abbey in 1537, **Ulverston** was regarded as the capital of Furness, a position enhanced by the opening of the Ulverston Canal in 1795. Though sadly no longer navigable, the canal once claimed to be the deepest, widest and shortest in the UK, at about 1¼ miles (1.75km) in length. It ran from Hammerside Hill on the Leven Estuary, an inlet of Morecambe Bay, to terminate at a basin and wharves in Ulverston, and featured a 112-foot (34-metre) sea lock. Today the towpath allows a pleasant stroll towards the coast, where the Bay Horse Hotel stands at the

Top left: **GRANGE-OVER-SANDS** The carefully restored station, and its commemorative plaque.

Left: **GRANGE-OVER-SANDS** The Ornamental Gardens next to the railway station.

Above: **KENTS BANK** An FR postcard, circa 1910.

Below: **ULVERSTON** Seen here in 1974, the imposing station at Ulverston was completed in 1878 at a cost of £10,000, to replace the previous inadequate facilities that formed the terminus of the original line from Barrow. It features an unusual arrangement of platforms that permitted direct transfer between main-line and Lakeside branch trains. For many years the station displayed a large sign proclaiming it to be the junction for Windermere Lakeside and Conishead Priory, although the passenger service to the latter was withdrawn in 1916.

water's edge on the Leven Estuary to welcome you. Here also is the long-distance footpath known as the Cumbria Coastal Way, a 185-mile (298km) route from Cumbria's southern edge to just beyond the Scottish border.

The canal was once a vital part of the town's economy, but its profitability declined with the opening of the railway. The

An extract from an 1896 Furness Railway Map

Furness Railway eventually bought the canal and, although it continued to be used commercially until the First World War, it was later abandoned. Spanning the canal is what is believed to be the only surviving 'rolling bridge' in England, built to carry the FR's branch line south to Conishead Priory in 1883. The design allowed the bridge to roll back into a small dock, leaving a central navigable channel for boats. A tall brick accumulator tower stands nearby, which housed the large water-filled pipe needed to operate the rams that moved the bridge. The bridge was granted Grade II listed status in January 2012. The walkway along the canal's eastern side is maintained by Ulverston Town Council. Further information can be obtained from

Above: **ULVERSTON** Passing Ulverston signal box in 1974, Stanier 'Black 5' No 44932 pilots Gresley 'A3' No 4472 *Flying Scotsman*. Following the lifting of the 'steam ban' on the national network in 1972, imposed by BR in 1968 for all steam locos except No 4472 (which had a contract to operate until 1970), a series of 'test runs' from Carnforth to Ulverston were operated by No 44932 and sister loco 44871. After their successful completion, there followed a number of 'steam specials' to Barrow-in-Furness, of which this was one.

Right: **ULVERSTON** This is the view along the Ulverston Canal from the sea lock. The canal borders the giant factory of Glaxo-Smith-Klein, which kindly donated the FR bench situated beside the towpath.

An extract from an 1896 Furness Railway

the Friends of Ulverston Canal at www. ulverstoncanalfriend.com.

At Ulverston, passengers taking the Furness Railway tour would have changed trains to follow the Lakeside branch and perhaps visit Newby Bridge or Conishead Priory (to which a branch line had been opened in 1883 as part of a plan to build a new line to Barrow, bypassing Ulverston and the steep climb to the summit at Lindal). This would entail first retracing their journey as far as the nearby triangular junction at Plumpton, there turning north via Greenodd and on to Haverthwaite, Newby Bridge Halt and Lakeside on Windermere, or south to Conishead Priory. Unfortunately, British Railways closed the Haverthwaite line to passengers in 1965

and to all traffic two years later, so visitors today must take the bus from Victoria Road (5 minutes from the station) for the short 10-minute ride to Haverthwaite railway station. The 518 Barrow-Windermere-Ambleside service operated by Travellers Choice and the 6 or X6 Barrow-Kendal service by Stagecoach both stop at Haverthwaite station.

The Conishead Priory branch (the rest of the line to Barrow was never built) was also eventually lifted and little evidence of its existence is now visible, except for the bridge over the Ulverston Canal. The Priory and its former station are now privately owned and not open to the public.

At **Haverthwaite** we change to the 3½-mile (5.5km) restored section of the route, which is now operated by the Lakeside & Haverthwaite Railway. Closed by BR in 1965 and

reopened as a heritage line in 1973 in a ceremony performed by the late Eric Treacy, then Bishop of Wakefield, it is now operational between March and November and features a variety of lovingly restored steam and diesel locomotives. It was originally opened from Plumpton Junction with great ceremony on 1 June 1869 to carry coal for the Windermere steamers, iron ore for Backbarrow Ironworks and sulphur and saltpetre for Black Beck and Low Wood gunpowder works, while in the other direction pig-iron, gunpowder, pit props, ultramarine and wooden bobbins were being carried from the Finsthwaite area. Before the FR arrived, flat-bottomed shallow-draft boats called 'Flatties' were used to carry the gunpowder from just above Low Wood bridge, down the River Leven to the estuary at Greenodd, which was then a thriving port serving Morecambe Bay. Today a public footpath through woods from Haverthwaite crosses the site of the former gunpowder works, where a well-preserved building with a clock tower dating from 1849 can still be seen. With the decline of the iron ore industry around the turn of the 20th century, attention turned instead to the rapidly growing tourist industry carrying day-trippers and holidaymakers to the vessels plying up and down Windermere.

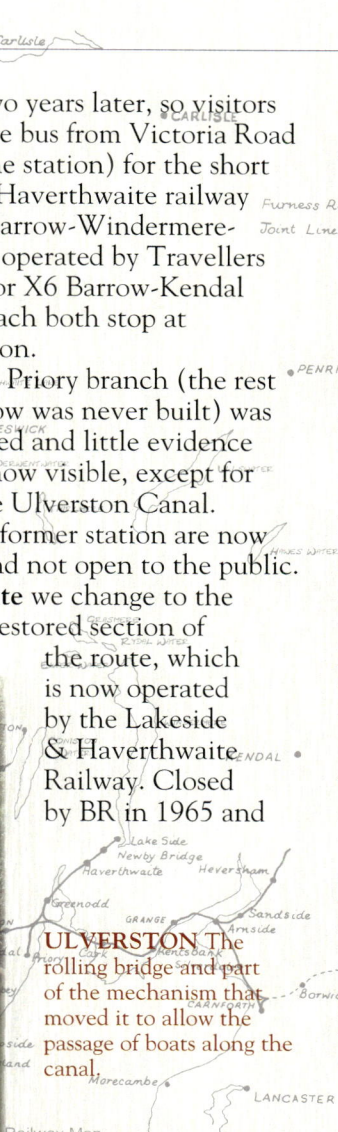

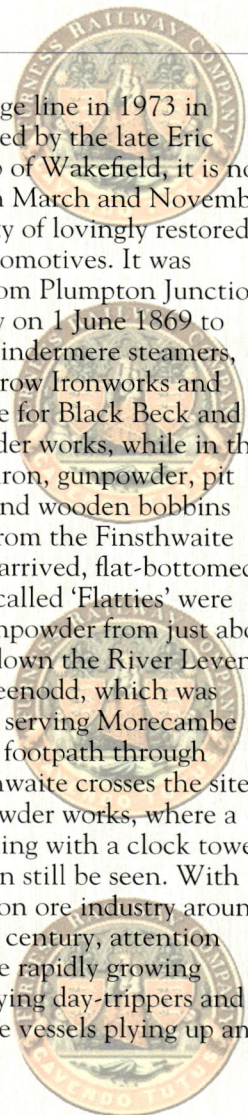

ULVERSTON The rolling bridge and part of the mechanism that moved it to allow the passage of boats along the canal.

BACKBARROW The site of the former Backbarrow Ironworks, seen here in April 2014, is now in the process of being redeveloped to provide luxury homes with studio/workshop space.

LOW WOOD This well-preserved clock tower stands on the site of the former gunpowder works at Low Wood. Here the horses that pulled the gunpowder vans along the narrow-gauge line to Haverthwaite station (no locomotives being allowed in the works for obvious reasons) were shod with either brass or copper shoes to eliminate the risk of a spark that might cause an explosion. It is possible that the rails on the site were also of non-ferrous metal. At Haverthwaite, the materials were transhipped to and from standard-gauge vehicles on the FR's Lakeside branch. The only steam engine on the site, still there as late as 1974, intact but rusty, was the stationary steam engine in the Power House. The mill closed in 1935 but the remains of some buildings still stand, and almost all the underground workings, the clock tower and the saltpetre refinery are perfectly preserved, being used now by several small businesses.

A short distance from Haverthwaite beside the A590 towards Newby Bridge on the River Leven is the village of **Backbarrow**. The valley has over the centuries featured many industries including corn mills, a dye works, cotton mills, gunpowder mills, an acid plant, bobbin and woollen mills, an iron-smelting furnace, a paper mill, a fulling mill and the ultramarine factory, as well as a host of more modest family businesses. They were of course established because of the abundant water power available from this outflow from Windermere.

An extract from an 1896 Furness Railway Map

The intensely cobalt-blue pigment 'ultramarine' or 'dolly blue', sold for use in washing to give a 'whiter than white' look to laundry, dyed the material a very faint shade of blue, which made it appear extremely white. The ultramarine powder was also used for whitening paper and in Tate & Lyle sugar – 'whitened with arsenic-free blue'! The 'Blue Mill', as it was known locally, was the source of the dust that gave much of the village a blue tint. Its commercial success was due in no small measure to the plentiful supply of water from the adjacent River Leven (for power and for washing the product) and its proximity to Haverthwaite railway station, which was connected to the main line through Ulverston, allowing quick and easy transport of raw materials and coal inwards and the finished product outwards to the UK and overseas.

The Blue Mill was in two portions connected by a narrow-gauge tramway that crossed the A590, with its trucks usually being propelled by works staff. Production ceased in 1981 and the mill finally closed the following year when modern detergents put an end to the 'dolly-blue bag' after more than a century of use. The Blue Dye Works

carton packaging sheds have a new lease of life as the home for the Lakeland Motor Museum, which relocated here from Holker Hall in 2010. It houses possibly one of the finest collections of automobilia on public display in the UK. For more information, see www.lakelandmotormuseum.co.uk.

In the same year, the mill itself was refurbished and relaunched as the Whitewater Hotel and Leisure Club, and a display of machinery from the mill is maintained on the premises, together with photographs of the former factory in operation.

After leaving Haverthwaite on a testing climb of 1 in 78, and with a high rock face to our left, the line plunges into East

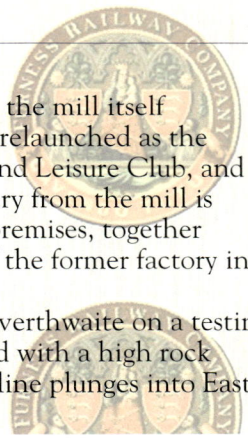

BACKBARROW The Whitewater Hotel celebrates its industrial heritage both inside and out.

Machinery on display in the Dolly Blue Bar area.

Traces of the blue dust still adorn the stonework in places, while machinery such as the turbine that produced all the mechanical power for the manufacturing process and the pulveriser are proudly displayed. Many thanks to the Manager and his staff for their assistance and permission to photograph on the premises.

Tunnel while still climbing steadily before emerging to take a sharp left-hand curve at the now easier grade of 1 in 120 and passing the ruins of Backbarrow Ironworks. A fine view over the Leven Valley can be enjoyed here, with the river and waterfall, while beyond is the former ultramarine works, now converted to the Lakeland Village and Whitewater Hotel. Still climbing, after a short straight section we round a long right-hand curve to pass under a bridge at Linstey Green, with the high mass of Gummers How Peak in the distance. Crossing the Finsthwaite road at Cuckoo Bridge, we are flanked by forests on one side and pasture for sheep and beef cattle on the other. After a long straight stretch we enter a deep cutting that opens out to reveal across the fields a waterfall below an old converted watermill, as we enter Newby Bridge station.

Passing under the Lakeside to Haverthwaite road, we descend through a cutting to the shores of Windermere, passing the impressive cast-iron Landing How Bridge, the slipway and winch house used by the Steamboat Company to haul its boats out of the water for maintenance. The journey to Lakeside (usually spelled Lake Side before preservation) behind a lovingly restored steam locomotive has brought us to the terminus at **Lakeside**

Pier at the southern end of Windermere. Moored alongside the platform of Lakeside station, with its large signal box at one end, is the boat that will take us up the lake to Bowness. The station is home to the Lakes Aquarium, and there is a restaurant on the pier offering panoramic views. For further information and timetables, please visit www.lakesiderailway.co.uk.

The train is met by a vessel such as the elegant MV *Swan* or *Teal*, now operated by Windermere Lake Cruises, although

Right: **LAKESIDE**
An FR postcard of the 'Lake Side Refreshment Pavilion', circa 1910.

Below: Controlling train movements at Lakeside station is the imposing signal box, and beyond it a lattice-post lower-quadrant semaphore signal.

Bagnall 0-6-0ST No 14 *Princess*, formerly of Preston Docks, has arrived at Lakeside station from Haverthwaite, giving passengers the opportunity to thank the loco's crew…

An extract from an 1896 Furness Railway Map

An extract from an 1896 Furness Railway Map

...before embarking on the next stage of their journey, aboard perhaps the MV *Teal* or MV *Swan*. Four modern motor ships now operate on Windermere, of which *Swan*, *Swift* and *Tern* are reconstructions of the former FR steam yachts bearing those honoured names, while *Teal* is a new addition; *Cygnet* sadly is no more.

WINDERMERE 'On Steam Yacht "Swift", Windermere', an FR postcard of 1902. *Ken Norman Collection*

this also was once part of the Furness Railway empire, having been bought from the Windermere United Steam Yacht Company, which had been operating on the lake since the 1840s. During the voyage to Bowness we are treated to magnificent views of mountain scenery, secluded bays and the many wooded islands that decorate this beautiful lake.

The *Illustrated Guide to the Holiday Resorts on the Furness Railway*, originally published in 1900, describes the lake steamer's destination of **Bowness-on-Windermere** as 'perhaps the most popular lake resort in the tourist and holiday season', referring to it as a 'quaint and curiously constructed town' with a 'labyrinth of small streets of maze-like formation'. Bowness is still recognised as the centre of the principal yachting and boating stations on the lake.

Above the arrival point at Bowness Pier stands the impressive Belsfield Hotel,

WINDERMERE, hailed as 'The Queen of the English Lakes', is also the longest, and a favourite among those who love to get out on the water. In Furness Railway days several steam boats made a daily circuit of the lake and the competition between them resulted in surprisingly low fares. In the early 1850s, for example, the advertised fare for a sail – a circuit of about 23 miles amid 'the most delicious scenery imaginable' – was a snip at only threepence.

overlooking the bay from its elevated position. It was once the home of Henry Schneider, Barrow Steelworks Chairman and co-founder of the Furness Railway Company. He would travel daily from here on his private steam yacht, the *Esperance* (now preserved in the Windermere Steamboat Museum) to Lakeside, there to board his private carriage on his railway line down to Barrow.

From Bowness Pier up the hill to **Windermere** is a walk of about 20 minutes, although an excellent bus service from the Pier connects the two towns, which, although they have now grown together, have both retained their own town centres

An extract from an 1896 Furness Railway Map

and thus their own identities. Windermere town is about half a mile (800 metres) up from the lake after which it was named, surrounded by picturesque mountain scenery.

The railway arrived at the town in 1847 as the Kendal & Windermere Railway, a branch from the Lancaster & Carlisle Railway at Oxenholme, built originally as a local enterprise as part of plans to continue the line northwards and on to Scotland. This ambitious project was thwarted by strong local opposition, not least from the poet William Wordsworth, who considered that the scheme would bring about an unwanted deterioration in the quality of life in this unspoilt and tranquil area of his beloved Lake District. Windermere is thus the terminus of the branch, which soon became part of the expanding network of the London & North Western Railway, and it is by means of this line that we now make our way back towards our starting point, although as mentioned earlier no West Coast Main Line trains now call at Carnforth station, so it will be necessary to travel on south to Lancaster, 10 minutes up the line, before returning northwards to our final destination. First TransPennine Express operates the Windermere branch trains from Windermere to Oxenholme, calling at Staveley, Burneside and Kendal. In addition there is the less regular service to Manchester Airport, which may be preferred as it requires no change of trains at Oxenholme and offers a journey time of about 35 minutes to Lancaster, compared

Above right: **BOWNESS-ON-WINDERMERE** 'The Promenade, Bowness-on-Windermere', from a postcard of about 1900.

Right: **BOWNESS-ON-WINDERMERE** The view up the lake from the garden of the Belsfield Hotel, with Bowness Pier in the foreground.

An extract from an 1896 Furness Railway Map

with 45 to 60 minutes, depending on the connection at Oxenholme.

The single-line branch from the now much reduced station at Windermere, where the simple facilities cater for passengers while the former main buildings are now home to a branch of a supermarket chain, follows the route of the A591 road to Kendal, a journey of about 15 minutes. It travels alongside the lovely River Gowan, first to **Staveley**, below the looming mass of Hugill Fell, where the Gowan joins the River Kent at the mouth of the Kentmere Valley. The village centre is now largely a Conservation Area with several listed buildings.

Passing through pleasant Lakeland countryside we come next to the small village of **Burneside** (pronounced 'Burnie Side'), with its single platform on your left-hand side. Here is the site of the ruined Burneside Hall, now a Grade II listed building. Mentioned in records dating back to 1290, the structure is a converted piel tower, a kind of watch tower where signal fires could be lit by the garrison to warn of approaching danger.

We cross the River Kent before continuing to the large market town of **Kendal**, the third largest town in Cumbria after Carlisle and Barrow-in-Furness. Nicknamed the 'Auld Grey Town' as a

result of its buildings being constructed with the local grey limestone, Kendal is the major tourist gateway to the Lake District, and home of the famous Mint Cake. This glucose-based confectionery has long been favoured as an energy food by walkers, explorers and mountaineers, having been carried on expeditions to the highest and the most remote places on earth. Among the town's many places of interest is Kendal Castle, dating back to the 12th century, and the Kendal Museum, one of the oldest in the country.

Nearby at Grayrigg is 'Animal Rescue Cumbria – the Wainwright Shelter', a charity that rescues and cares for cats and dogs, finding them new homes whenever possible. Influential guidebook author Alfred Wainwright MBE (1907-91) gave most of the profits from his books to animal charities, and in 1972 became Chairman of this charity.

Travelling on, climbing by a tortuous bend from the valley, we reach **Oxenholme**, whose station was originally called Kendal Junction but now rejoices in the name Oxenholme Lake District, for here the Windermere branch joins the West Coast Main Line, where connections can be made to Carlisle and Scotland to the north and Lancaster to the south. As previously noted, trains from Windermere

terminate here (except those to Manchester Airport), requiring passengers to change to the main-line express trains currently operated by Virgin Trains for the onward journey to Lancaster. The journey time from Oxenholme to Lancaster is less than 20 minutes, and less again if aboard the faster Virgin Trains service destined for London Euston. From Lancaster, the regular First TransPennine Express service back to Carnforth takes about 10 minutes and concludes our journey following the Furness Railway's Circular Tour Number 3.

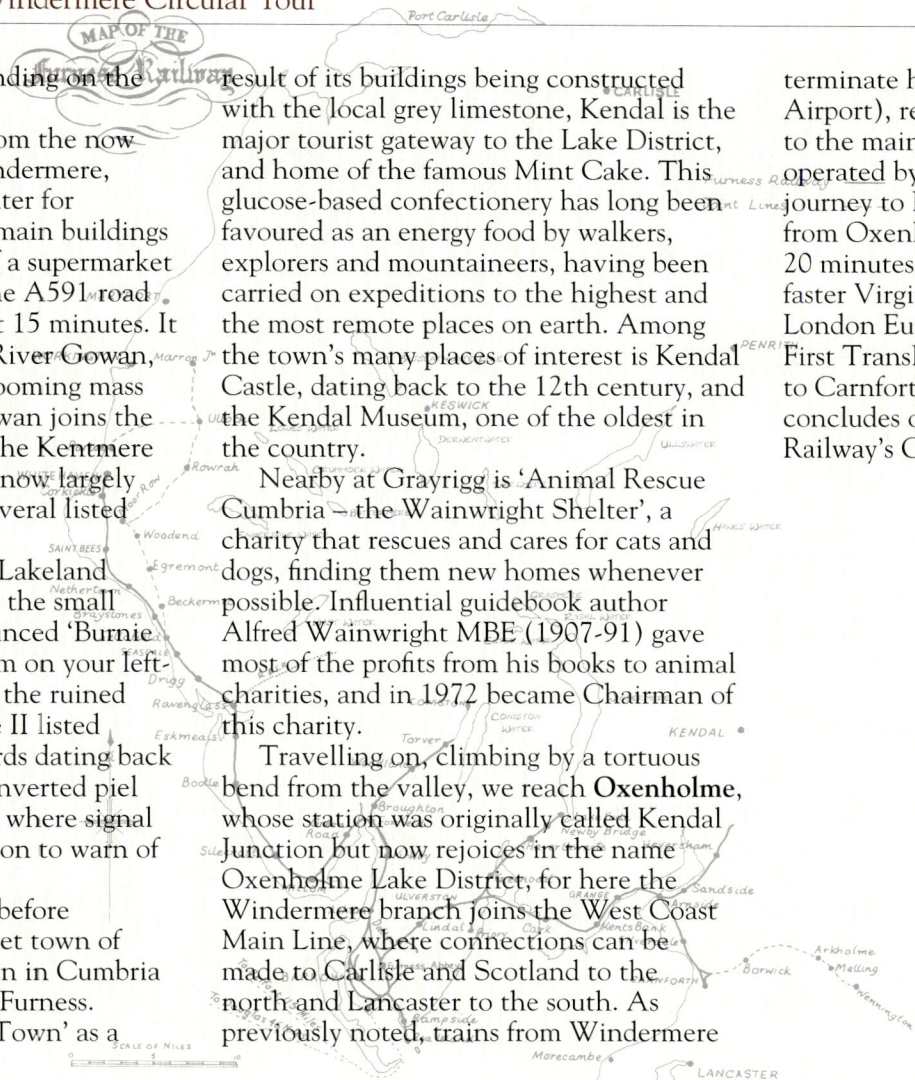

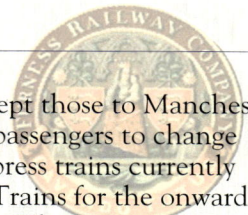

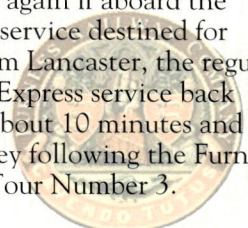

An extract from an 1896 Furness Railway Map

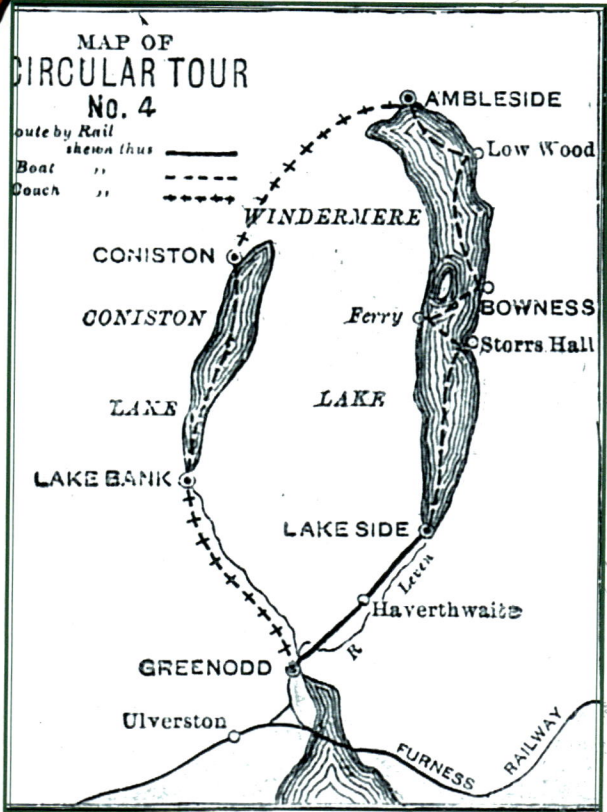

MAP OF
CIRCULAR TOUR
NO. 4

Route by Rail
shewn thus ____
Boat   ,,   ------
Coach   ,,   ++++++

AMBLESIDE
Low Wood
WINDERMERE
CONISTON
CONISTON
Ferry
BOWNESS
Storrs Hall
LAKE
LAKE
LAKE BANK
LAKE SIDE
Haverthwaite
GREENODD
Ulverston
FURNESS RAILWAY

Tour 4: The Middle Circular Tour
Ambleside-Bowness-Lakeside-Haverthwaite-Greenodd-Coniston-Ambleside

By boat from Ambleside to Lakeside heritage railway to Haverthwaite – bus to Lake Bank via Greenodd – boat to Coniston – bus to Ambleside

- Allow about 8½ hours for the full itinerary (can be shortened)
- Suggested staring point: Ambleside

Tour 4: Typical journey times

By boat
dep Ambleside 09.50 to Lakeside
   (approx 80 mins)
By rail (L&HR)
dep Lakeside 11.15 to Haverthwaite
   (approx 20 mins)
By bus (X6)
dep Haverthwaite 11.47 to Greenodd
   (approx 6 mins)
By bus (X12)
dep Greenodd 12.27 to Lake Bank
   (approx 20 mins)
Picnic lunch at Lake Bank
By boat
dep Lake Bank 13.35 to Coniston
   (approx 50 mins)

By bus (505)
Coniston dep 14.43 to Ambleside
   (approx 50 mins)

Alternatively remain on the X12 bus from Greenodd as far as Torver, arriving 12.49, and have lunch. Walk down the lane to the lake (about 20 mins from the village centre), from where boats to Coniston run hourly. Or if you prefer a walk, take the lakeside footpath and road from Lake Bank to Torver (about 3½ miles), then by boat from there to Coniston (approx 25 mins).

Note: Bus, rail and ferry timetables can change at very short notice. Be sure to check details before travelling.

An extract from an 1896 Furness Railway Map

WINDERMERE seen from Low Wood, circa 1910

LAKESIDE PIER Passengers arriving by boat at Lakeside Pier can transfer easily to the adjacent railway to continue their journey to Haverthwaite.

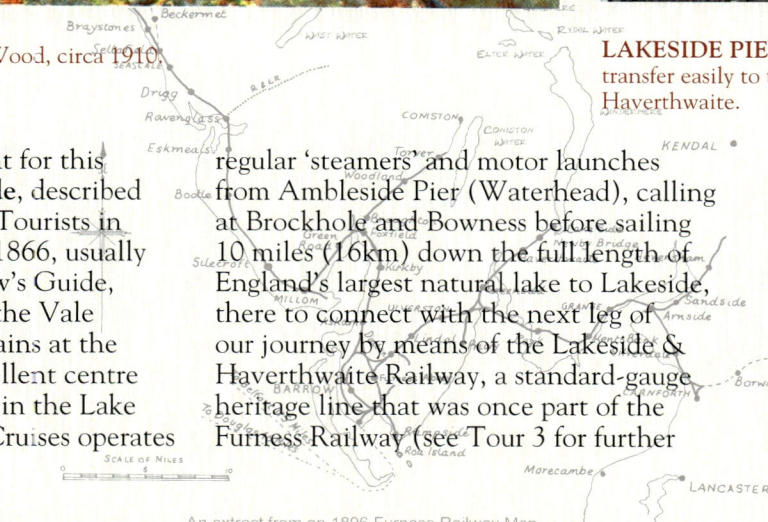

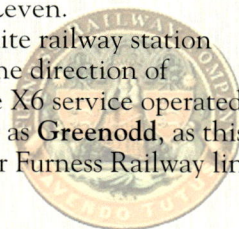

A convenient starting point for this circular tour is **Ambleside**, described in Bradshaw's Handbook for Tourists in Great Britain and Ireland of 1866, usually simply referred to as Bradshaw's Guide, as 'a charming little town in the Vale of Brathay among the mountains at the head of Windermere, an excellent centre for excursions short and long in the Lake District.' Windermere Lake Cruises operates regular 'steamers' and motor launches from Ambleside Pier (Waterhead), calling at Brockhole and Bowness before sailing 10 miles (16km) down the full length of England's largest natural lake to Lakeside, there to connect with the next leg of our journey by means of the Lakeside & Haverthwaite Railway, a standard-gauge heritage line that was once part of the Furness Railway (see Tour 3 for further details). The terminus station at **Lakeside Pier** affords an easy transfer to a steam hauled train for the 20-minute ride to **Haverthwaite**, following the lovely wooded valley of the River Leven.

From Haverthwaite railway station we take the bus in the direction of Ulverston, using the X6 service operated by Stagecoach as far as **Greenodd**, as this section of the former Furness Railway line

An extract from an 1896 Furness Railway Map

Old Man of Coniston, as well as slate and iron, to Nibthwaite. Here cargoes could be transhipped by road to Greenodd, then an important port and shipbuilding centre, for forwarding by sea. This all ended with the coming of the trains, simultaneously capturing the road traffic and opening the way for the development of the tourist industry. The Furness Railway was quick to

WINDERMERE 'Summer's Day, Waterhead (Windermere)', reproduced from *The English Lake Land* by G. P. Abraham, published in Keswick in 1922.

LAKESIDE PIER *Passengers transfer between Miss Lakeland II, operated by Windermere Lake Cruises, and the Lakeside & Haverthwaite Railway.*

sadly no longer exists. At Greenodd, opposite the Texaco garage, change to the X12 Apollo 8 service from Ulverston to Coniston, now travelling northwards along the valley of the River Crayke as far as **Lake Bank**, a quiet and unspoilt corner of the South Lakes just a 1-minute walk from the shore of Coniston Water and the jetty operated by the Coniston Launch Company.

Before the arrival of the railway, **Coniston Water** had long been used for the transport of copper ore from the slopes of The

An extract from an 1896 Furness Railw

realise the potential of a steamer service on the lake, and in 1859 launched its newly acquired steam yacht, which it named *Gondola* on account of her elegant shape recalling the style of the Venetian canal boats. *Gondola* sailings ran in connection with the arrival of trains at Coniston station, but when the company's freight traffic increased as a result of the rapid expansion of Barrow's iron and steel industry, passenger train punctuality deteriorated, so in 1870 Henry Cook, the FR's Traffic Manager, introduced the first 'Circular Tours of Lakeland', integrating rail, road and water transport. These would later be greatly extended by Alfred Aslett, the company's General Manager, who successfully persuaded the Board of the need for a second vessel for Coniston. *Lady of the Lake* was launched in 1907, and both vessels operated until the outbreak of the First World War. Sailings recommenced after the war, and later the LMS continued some of the Circular Tours, with the road sections being operated by Ribble Motors.

Gondola was 'retired' in 1939 and, after seemingly being wrecked and sunk, was saved by the National Trust and largely rebuilt and refurbished by Vickers of Barrow to an elegant standard reminiscent of the Victorian Age, returning to service in June 1980. Unfortunately no such happy

CONISTON A Furness Railway postcard of SY *Lady of the Lake* at Bank Pier.

outcome favoured *Lady of the Lake*, which continued in service until the outbreak of the Second World War, and was broken up for scrap in 1950.

The charming *Gondola* continues to sail daily throughout the summer season. The 50-minute cruise from Lake Bank to Coniston, which operates on Mondays and Thursdays from May to September only, gives ample opportunity to view this tranquil lake and its stunning shoreline. However, because of the limited timetable operated from Lake Bank, you may decide to omit this section of the cruise, opting

to continue on to Torver, about half way up the lake, by bus or on foot, to take advantage of the regular hourly sailings (March to November) from there to Coniston (see the 'Typical journey times' table above).

Coniston Water achieved more recent fame when Donald Campbell broke four World Water Speed Records on the lake in the 1950s. He is buried in the village's 'new' graveyard, having died here in an attempt to break the speed record for the eighth time in 1967 in his boat *Bluebird*.

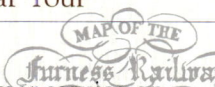

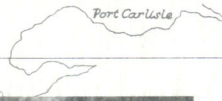

CONISTON The lovingly restored steam yacht *Gondola* arriving at Coniston jetty.

CONISTON FR postcard: 'Coniston Lake (Charcoal Burners)', circa 1910.

Coniston, a popular centre for hill-walking, nestles between the lake and The Old Man of Coniston. The village became popular with Victorian tourists thanks to the Furness Railway, which opened its 8½-mile (14km) single-track Coniston branch to passengers in 1859. It left the main line at Foxfield, near Broughton in Furness, and went by way of Woodland and Torver. Originally intended as a freight line to carry copper ore from the mines above Coniston, this turned out to be uncompetitive and

the line became increasingly dependent on tourism. The Furness Railway had begun its steamer services on the lake in 1860 with the steam yacht *Gondola*, and this was included in two of the company's original 'Circular Tours of Lakeland' introduced in 1870, later joined by the much large *Lady of the Lake*.

Coniston station was designed by the Lancaster architect E. G. Paley in the 'Swiss Chalet' style. It was enlarged between 1888 and 1892, and further by the addition of a

third platform in 1896. At about the same time, the loco shed (a 'sub-shed' to Barrow, coded 11B) was doubled in length and the goods shed was also enlarged.

Sadly this success did not last, as Coniston's somewhat isolated location made further development of tourism more challenging, especially during the period of austerity following the Second World War. Even the reintroduction by BR of Camping Coaches at Coniston, initiated by the LMS, failed to generate sufficient passenger

An extract from an 1896 Furness Railway Map

CONISTON The Bluebird Cafe at Coniston Launch provides a reminder of Donald Campbell's exploits on the lake.

numbers. Inevitably, and despite local objections, the line was closed to passenger traffic in October 1958, the first such closure in the Lake District. Goods traffic continued until April 1962 after which the line was abandoned. Coniston's handsome station buildings were demolished, although the footbridge was saved and re-erected at Ravenglass on the narrow-gauge Ravenglass & Eskdale Railway. The station buildings at Broughton, Woodland and Torver also all survive as private residences. (Please refer to Tour 2, The Inner Circular Tour, for more information about the Coniston Railway.)

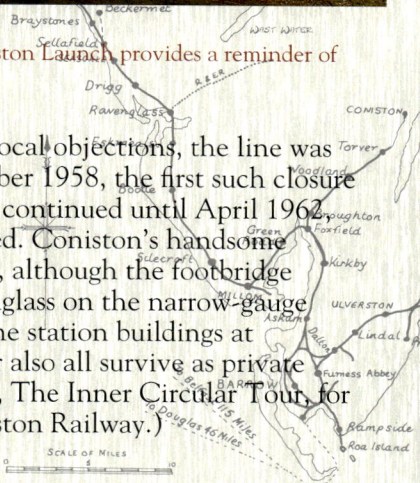

The Old Man of Coniston, at 2,634 feet (803 metres), was described by Alfred Wainwright in his classic *Pictorial Guide to the Lakeland Fells* as 'a benevolent giant, revered by generations of walkers', being the southernmost point of the high Lakelands, 'the last outpost, looking far over the sea'. He went on to observe that 'Although cruelly scarred and mutilated by quarrying, the Old Man has retained a dignified bearing, and still raises his proud and venerable head to the sky.'

CONISTON Ivatt 2MT 2-6-2T No 41217 stands at Coniston station in the early 1960s. This 'push-pull'-fitted loco was built at Crewe Works in September 1948 and shedded at Carlisle Kingmoor until being withdrawn in December 1966 and cut up at the scrap-yard of J. McWilliams, Shettleston, Glasgow, in September 1967. More than 200 locos met a similar fate in this yard, including Stanier 'Black 5s' and 'Jubilees', 'Britannias', 9Fs, Thompson 'A2s' and 'B1s'. Coniston station and the branch were closed to passengers in 1958 and to goods in 1962. *R. K. Blencowe*

Above: **CONISTON** A Furness railway postcard showing the Old Man of Coniston in about 1910.

Right: **CONISTON** The long climb to the summit of the Old Man, although steep in places, rewards those who reach the cairn with stunning views over South Lakeland.

Leaving the lake at Coniston, the regular 505 bus service to Windermere operated by Stagecoach takes us back to our starting point at Ambleside.

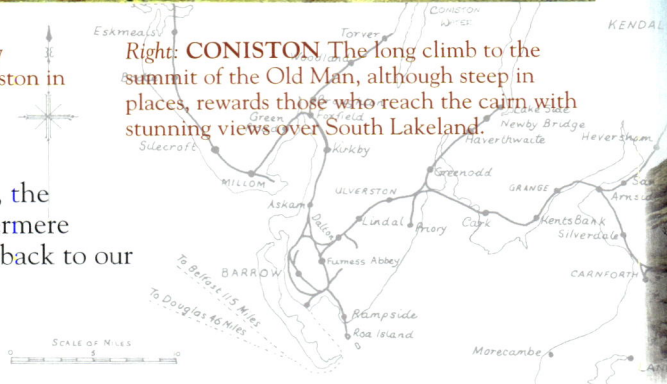

An extract from an 1896 Furness Railway Map

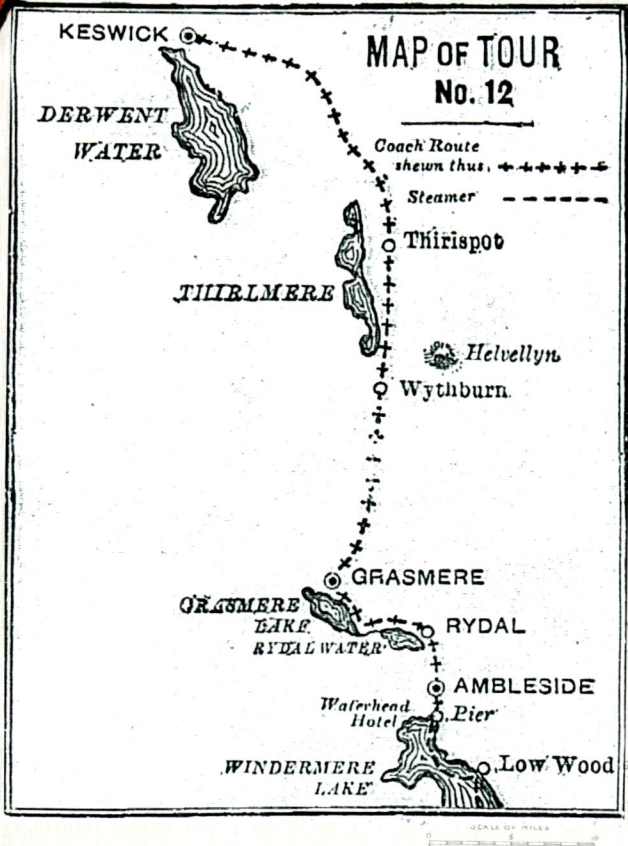

MAP OF TOUR No. 12

KESWICK

DERWENT WATER

Coach Route shewn thus +++++

Steamer – – – – –

Thirlspot

THIRLMERE

Helvellyn

Wythburn

GRASMERE

GRASMERE LAKE
RYDAL WATER

RYDAL

AMBLESIDE
Pier

Waterhead Hotel

WINDERMERE LAKE

Low Wood

SCALE OF MILES

An extract from an 1896 Furness Railway Map

Tour 12: The Derwentwater (Keswick) Tour

Ambleside-Rydal-Grasmere-Thirlmere-Keswick-Thirlmere-Grasmere-Rydal-Ambleside

By bus from Ambleside to Keswick and return

- Allow about 6 hours for the full itinerary (with option of additional 80-minute cruise)
- Suggested starting point: Keswick Road, Ambleside

Tour 12: Typical journey times

Outward
By bus (555)
dep Ambleside 09.22 to Keswick via Rydal, Grasmere and Thirlmere (approx 50 mins)
Buses leave hourly from Keswick Road, 5 mins from centre of village

Return
By bus (555)
dep 14.25 from Keswick bus station to White Lion Inn, Ambleside (approx 40 mins)
Buses, bound for Lancaster, leave hourly from Stand 2 at the bus station, and retrace the outward journey

Optional additional cruise
Boats from Ambleside, operated by Windermere Lake Cruises, sail at very regular intervals from Ambleside Pier (Waterhead) from 09.50 throughout the day until 18.20 in the season (earlier during later months). Last return from Bowness is 18.15 (also earlier during the later months). Ambleside to Bowness and return takes about 80 minutes.

Note: Bus, rail and ferry timetables can change at very short notice. Be sure to check details before travelling.

This return tour by bus between Ambleside and Keswick may be supplemented by beginning or ending with a cruise on Windermere from the terminal at Waterhead Pier. Operated by Windermere Lake Cruises, sailings depart at regular intervals during the season. The return journey to Bowness takes about 80 minutes.

The bus journey using service 555 operated by Stagecoach takes us alongside the charming lakes of Rydal Water, Grasmere and Thirlmere on our way to the popular tourist destination of Keswick, on Derwent Water. As there is such a regular bus service the journey can be broken and resumed along the way, giving the opportunity to further explore this exceptional area.

Ambleside is now a major tourist centre and a fine base for visiting the many places of interest in the area. Bradshaw's Guide recommends Stock Ghyll Force, 'a splendid waterfall on the stream which rises in the Kirkstone Fells and runs through Ambleside.' Only a short walk from the centre of the village, its cascade is well worth a short detour, as are the nearby Wansfell Pike and Skelgill, which

according to Bradshaw 'are easily ascended, but Fairfield, at 2,950 feet [885 metres], is more fatiguing, the prospect from which, however, is magnificent.'

The nearest railway station to Ambleside is 4 miles away at Windermere, which is connected by way of Kendal to the West Coast Main Line at Oxenholme (please refer to Tour 3, The Grange and Windermere Circular Tour, for more details). Plans for a railway line from Windermere to Ambleside, proposed in 1886, were refused by the LNWR on the grounds that the building costs were too great, so the idea was abandoned.

Travelling north from Ambleside, we quickly come upon **Rydal Water**, concisely but accurately described by Alfred Wainwright in his *Pictorial Guide to the Lakeland Fells* as 'a charming lake'. In a commanding position overlooking the lake is Nab Scar (1,450 feet [435 metres]), made well known by its association with the Lakeland Poets who came to dwell at

NAB SCAR The impressive bulk of Nab Scar. At its base, the River Rothay runs between Rydal Water and Windermere.

Above and above right: **RYDAL** Furness Railway postcards depicting 'The Stepping Stones, Rydal' and 'Rydal Water – frosty morning'.

Right: **Nr GRASMERE** A light aircraft flies along the valley just north of Grasmere, passing the well known landmark of the 'Lion and the Lamb'.

the foot of its steep, wooded slopes. According to Wainwright its association with romance and its fine abrupt height have made it a favourite with visitors. One of the smallest lakes in the Lake District, Rydal Water nevertheless plays an important part in the itinerary of the many tourists who climb the steps leading up from its western end to reach 'Wordsworth's Seat', reputedly the poet's favourite viewpoint.

Almost immediately after leaving Rydal Water we encounter **Grasmere** and its lake in an attractive vale, overlooked by one of the most recognisable landmarks in the Lake District, the 'Lion and

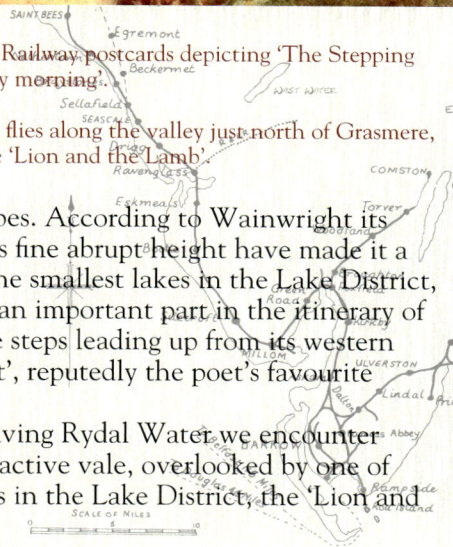

the Lamb' rock formations on the summit of Helm Crag. Famous worldwide for its Wordsworth connections, the village of Grasmere is the starting point for a number of popular walks that feature the picturesque River Rothay and, of course, Grasmere lake itself.

Continuing northwards we soon come to the reservoir of **Thirlmere**, created in 1894 from two smaller lakes by a dam that flooded the valley near the village of

Wythburn to provide drinking water for the growing conurbation of Manchester.

This is a favourite area for hill-walkers. Dunmail Raise is the highest point on the pass between Grasmere and Keswick, where the A591 road passes to the south of Thirlmere. Seat Sandall (2,415 feet [725 metres]) is prominent here, as are Dollywaggon Pike (2,810 feet [843 metres]) and Nethermost Pike (2,920 feet [876 metres]), trodden by the boots of thousands

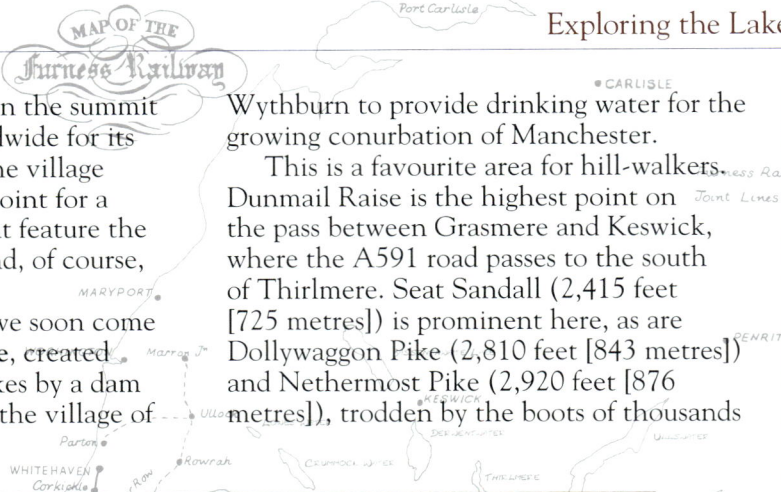

Above: **WYTHBURN** A horse-drawn coach pauses at Wythburn Church near the southern end of Thirlmere in about 1900. In an isolated position on the A591 Ambleside-Grasmere-Keswick road, there has been a church on this site on the eastern shore since 1554. It remains in active use in spite of the local population being severely reduced in the 19th century when the adjacent valley was flooded by Manchester Corporation to create Thirlmere Reservoir. The second view shows the church in May 2014.

Left: **GRASMERE** An FR postcard of Grasmere Church.

GRASMERE CHURCH.

AMBLESIDE STATION.

An extract from an 1896 Furness Railway Map

of pilgrims every year. In the words of Wainwright, 'it is the great magnet of Helvellyn which has drawn them here, and Nethermost Pike has been climbed incidentally, a mere obstacle in the route to its bigger neighbour.' Helvellyn is easily accessible and climbed more often than any other Lakeland mountain, 'a very friendly giant'. Wainwright goes on to describe how it inspires great affection, 'endearing it in the memory of its devotees, who return to it so often.' Having said that, it is a mountain with a summit of 3,118 feet (935 metres) and should be treated with respect. The Helvellyn range is indeed massive and forms a tremendous natural barrier between the deep troughs of the Thirlmere and Ullswater valleys. With this on our right or eastern side, we travel on, first north, then north-west to join the A66 road from Penrith towards our destination, the thriving market town of Keswick.

Keswick lies just north of Derwent Water and a short distance from Bassenthwaite Lake in the beautiful Vale of the Greta, below Skiddaw. The town is a major tourist centre, allowing easy access to picturesque valleys with lakes and unspoilt villages, and with the slopes of Skiddaw, Helvellyn and Scafell all within easy reach. Above the town is the most visited stone circle in Cumbria, a well preserved and atmospheric prehistoric monument at Castlerigg.

The short walk down to Derwent Water passes the Theatre by the Lake, whose productions have drawn much critical acclaim, while the views from the shore across to the imposing bulk

KESWICK Main Street, from a postcard by H. Webster, Helvellyn House, Keswick.

Leaving Keswick for Windermere. Skiddaw behind   Abraham's Series No. 420, Keswick.

Above: **CASTLERIGG** The ancient stone circle at Castlerigg, above Keswick.

Above right: **KESWICK** 'Leaving Keswick for Windermere, Skiddaw behind', from a postcard by Abraham, Series No 420, Keswick, circa 1900.

of Cat Bells attract countless visitors, as do the vantage points of Friar's Crag and Ashness. Not far from the town centre is the Cumberland Pencil Museum, Keswick

Left: **DERWENT WATER** is seen from Lower Falcon Crag, looking towards Keswick, with Bassenthwaite Lake beyond.

being the origin of the world's first graphite pencils.

Keswick was once on the railway that linked the Lake District's interior to the coast. The Cockermouth, Keswick & Penrith Railway (CK&PR) was a 31-mile (50km) line described by Bradshaw as 'passing through country remarkable for the grandeur of its sublimity'. The line closed in 1972 (see Tour 13, the Five Lakes Tour, for more details), but Keswick is now at the centre of a project the plans to reopen part of this once important rail route, mainly to re-establish the Penrith to Keswick section. For more information on this proposed

scheme, visit 'Keswick to Penrith Railway Reopening' at www.keswickrailway.com.

A few hours enjoying the pleasures of Keswick soon pass before the return bus journey to Ambleside via the same route. It is just as rewarding travelling south, allowing yet another perspective on the incomparable scenery.

Overleaf: **ASHNESS BRIDGE** with Derwent Water in the background.

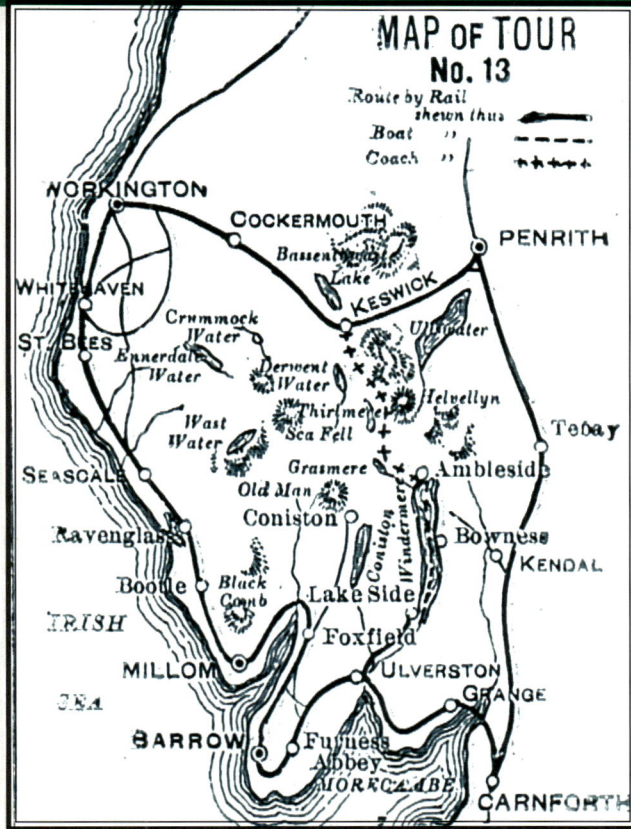

MAP OF TOUR No. 13

Route by Rail shewn thus
Boat "
Coach "

WORKINGTON
COCKERMOUTH
PENRITH
Bassenthwaite Lake
KESWICK
WHITEHAVEN
St. BEES
Crummock Water
Ullswater
Ennerdale Water
Derwent Water
Helvellyn
WAST Water
Thirlmere
Sca Fell
Tebay
SEASCALE
Grasmere
Old Man
Ambleside
RAVENGLASS
Coniston
Bowness
KENDAL
Bootle
Black Comb
Lake Side
IRISH SEA
Foxfield
MILLOM
ULVERSTON
GRANGE
BARROW
Furness Abbey
MORECAMBE
CARNFORTH

Tour 13: The Five Lakes Circular Tour

Ulverston-Lakeside-Ambleside-Thirlmere-Keswick-Cockermouth-Workington-Whitehaven-Ravenglass-Millom-Barrow-Ulverston
or
Ulverston-Lakeside-Ambleside-Thirlmere-Keswick-Penrith-Tebay-Lancaster-Carnforth-

Ulverston

By bus from Ulverston to Haverthwaite – heritage railway to Lakeside – boat to Bowness and Ambleside – bus to Keswick and Workington – national rail to Ulverston
or
By bus to Penrith and national rail to Ulverston via Lancaster and Carnforth

- Allow about 8 hours for the full itinerary (can be shortened)
- Suggested starting point: Ulverston railway station

WINDERMERE, and the northern area of Bowness and Ambleside in particular, attracts those who love boats and boating. Here an enthusiast tacks behind our steamer from Lakeside.

An extract from an 1896 Furness Railway Map

Tour 13: Typical journey times

By bus (X6)
dep Ulverston 09.52 to Haverthwaite
(approx 12 mins)
By rail (L&HR)
dep Haverthwaite 10.35 to Lakeside
(approx 20 mins)
By boat
dep Lakeside 11.20 to Bowness (approx 30 mins)
By boat
dep Bowness 12.20 to Ambleside (approx 30 mins)
By bus (555)
dep Ambleside 13.22 to Keswick (approx 50 mins)
By bus (X5)
dep Keswick 14.45 to Workington (approx 65 mins)

By rail
dep Workington 16.02 to Ulverston
(approx 80 mins)
or
By bus (X4/X5)
dep Keswick 14.20 to Penrith (approx 45 mins)
By rail
dep Penrith 15.45 to Lancaster (approx 40 mins)
By rail
dep Lancaster 16.55 to Ulverston (approx 45 mins)

Note: Bus, rail and ferry timetables can change at very short notice. Be sure to check details before travelling.

This circular tour visits the five lakes encountered on Tour 12 but includes either the train journey along the beautiful Cumbrian Coast line or a trip on the West Coast Main Line over the famous Shap summit, together with the opportunity to ride a steam-hauled train on the preserved Lakeside & Haverthwaite Railway.

Start your journey at **Ulverston** and follow the route described in Tour 3, the Grange and Windermere Circular Tour (page 19), to **Lakeside Pier** at the southern end of Windermere, then board a Windermere Lake Cruises boat to sail the full length of England's longest lake via Bowness to **Ambleside Pier** (Waterhead).

For the journey on from Ambleside, follow the route described in Tour 12, the Derwentwater (Keswick) Tour (page 45), travelling by bus to Keswick.

At Keswick there is a choice to be made. The preferred route is to head west by bus to Workington on the coast, then south along the wonderful Cumbrian Coast line via Barrow-in-Furness back to Ulverston. An alternative, particularly if time is short, is to travel east by bus from Keswick to Penrith to join the West Coast Main Line for the return journey to Ulverston via Lancaster, as detailed in Tour 3 (see page 37).

The important and popular town of **Keswick** lies approximately half way between the Irish Sea coast at Workington and Penrith, the strategic junction with the London & North Western Railway

WINDERMERE All along the shore, small rowing boats and self-drive motor boats can be hired by the hour.

and beyond. The railway connecting these two points was owned and operated by the Cockermouth & Workington Railway (C&WR) and the Cockermouth, Keswick & Penrith Railway (CK&PR), Keswick being the headquarters of the latter.

Following the preferred route westwards (see below for the alternative easterly route), the first part of our journey follows the line of the CK&PR. The railway was opened in 1865 and served several intermediate stations. The initial impetus for its construction was to bring high-grade coking coal from County Durham to the iron-ore smelting industry of West Cumberland, but it was not long before tourism became important and the trains brought day-trippers flocking to Keswick, much to the annoyance of those who preferred to maintain the town's genteel image. Although an independent company, the CK&PR never operated its own trains, these being run by the LNWR for passengers and goods, and the North Eastern Railway (NER) for the mineral traffic, which carried on beyond Penrith by means of the Eden Valley line. As visitor numbers continued to increase it became necessary to double the line over much of the section from Penrith. The 1920s then saw the introduction of the Lake District's most famous summer train, the 'Lakes Express', which ran from London Euston to Windermere and had a Keswick portion that soon comprised up to three coaches. This service ran until 1965.

However, as improvements were made to the process of coke-making, West Cumberland coal became more widely used and by 1910 the use of Durham coal was in decline, the traffic in this commodity disappearing completely by the mid-1920s. The line's viability declined further as private car use increased from the mid-1950s, and the section west of Keswick was closed in 1966, followed by the remainder of the CK&PR in 1972. However, a scheme is under way to reinstate the eastern stretch of the line between Keswick and Penrith as a modern railway, once again linking this part of the Lake District with the national rail network. For more information on this proposal, visit 'Keswick to Penrith Railway Reopening' at www.keswickrailway.com.

Much of the former railway route is now traced by the A66 road. Along the way some of the buildings of the intermediate stations can still be seen. The impressive main station buildings at Keswick have been preserved and restored and are now in use as the Keswick Country House Hotel. At **Braithwaite** sections of the trackbed can be discerned, especially a low embankment where it crosses the A66 north-east of

COCKERMOUTH, KESWICK, AND PENRITH RAILWAY.

Cumberland Lakes & Mountains

Lakes: Derwentwater, Buttermere, Crummock, Ullswater, Thirlmere, and Bassenthwaite.

Mountains: Skiddaw, Helvellyn, Scafell, &c., &c.

Golf Links: Embleton, 18 Holes. Keswick, 9 Holes.

THIS Railway affords the readiest access to the heart of the Lake District, and is in immediate connection with trains to all parts. Through arrangements with the London & North Western, North Eastern, Midland, Furness, and other Railways.

TOURIST TICKETS from all principal Stations to Keswick, Troutbeck (for Ullswater), and Cockermouth.

CIRCULAR TOURS from Cockermouth and Keswick Stations to Patterdale (Ullswater), **Windermere, Ambleside,** &c., by Rail, Coach, and Boats.

COACHES run between Troutbeck Station and **Patterdale** (Ullswater), daily during the Summer months.

COACHES leave Keswick Station daily for Borrowdale and Buttermere over Honister Pass, passing on the way Barrow and Lodore Waterfalls, and allowing sufficient time at Buttermere for visiting Scale Force Waterfall.

Particulars of Arrangements and Bookings on Company's Announcements.

J. CLARK, Secretary and Manager,

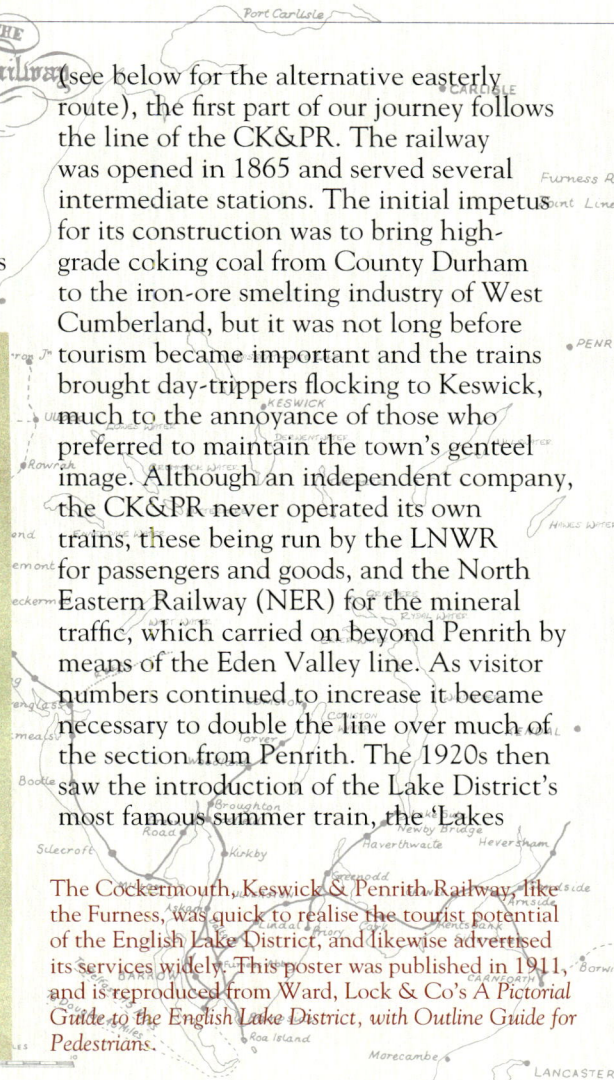

The Cockermouth, Keswick & Penrith Railway, like the Furness, was quick to realise the tourist potential of the English Lake District, and likewise advertised its services widely. This poster was published in 1911, and is reproduced from Ward, Lock & Co's A Pictorial Guide to the English Lake District, with Outline Guide for Pedestrians.

Above: **KESWICK** The Keswick Hotel features the platform and some of the buildings of the town's former station, with the trackbed now a cycleway/footpath alongside. The station, on the former Cockermouth, Keswick & Penrith Railway, was opened on 2 January 1865 and closed to goods traffic from 1 June 1964, and all traffic westwards ceased on 18 April 1966. It became an unstaffed halt from 1 July 1968 and finally closed to passengers on 6 March 1972. It is located immediately to the north of the town – follow the brown signs to 'Leisure Pool'.

Top right: **BASSENTHWAITE LAKE** reproduced from *The English Lake Land* by G. P. Abraham, published in Keswick in 1922.

Right: **BASSENTHWAITE LAKE** from Sale Fell.

An extract from an 1896 Furness Railway M

Keswick, while at **Embleton** the Station House still stands beside the road to Cockermouth.

Take the X5 service bus (operated by Stagecoach) from Stand 3 at Keswick bus station to Workington. This scenic route skirts one of the Lake District's largest lakes, **Bassenthwaite Lake**. It is the only body of water in the Lake District to be technically defined as a 'lake', and to use that word in its name – all the others are 'waters', 'meres' or 'tarns'.

Bassenthwaite Lake is a National Nature Reserve owned and managed by the Lake District National Park. Since 2001 it has been the home of the Lake District Osprey Project, centred in Dodd Wood, 3 miles (5km) north of Keswick off the A591. There are two open-air viewpoints manned by volunteers with powerful 'scopes' each day during the 'Osprey season', from April to September, after which the birds migrate to their winter home in Africa. The Bassenthwaite ospreys have recolonised England naturally as part of their population expansion from Scotland. The last time ospreys nested in England was more than 150 years ago, at about the time the Furness Railway was beginning to establish itself in the Barrow area. The Lake District Osprey Project is a partnership between the Forestry Commission and the

RSPB, with the support of the Lake District National Park. For more information, visit www.ospreywatch.co.uk/wordpress.

There is a car park with toilets, and refreshments can be taken at the Old Sawmill Tearoom, where you will also find leaflets describing a number of Forestry Commission walks where you can look out for red squirrels. The nearby Whinlatter Forest is a red squirrel stronghold managed by the Forestry Commission and the Red Squirrel North of England Project to help secure the long-term survival of the species in Cumbria.

Close by is the historic country manor of Mirehouse, whose house and gardens are also open to the public on certain days each week – see www.mirehouse.com for opening times and admission charges. Its entrance is opposite Dodd Wood car park and the car parking charge for Dodd Wood is refundable against admission to Mirehouse.

If time permits, the elegant Armathwaite Hall Hotel and Spa, off the quiet B5291 at the northern end of Bassenthwaite, is in an ideal location to treat oneself to afternoon tea overlooking the lovely lake.

The bus journey continues to the market town of **Cockermouth**, birthplace of William Wordsworth. Here you can see

BASSENTHWAITE LAKE A male osprey swoops above the surface of Bassenthwaite Lake on the hunt for a fish supper to be shared with his mate back at the nearby nest site.

DODD WOOD A red squirrel.

the partly ruined remains of the Norman castle, where Mary Queen of Scots was held prisoner in 1568, although the site is only open to the public on special occasions such as during the Cockermouth Festival in July.

Following the valley of the River Derwent we come to the former coal port and market town of **Workington**, described in Bradshaw's Guide as 'belonging to the Curwens of Workington Hall, a fine old seat, in which Mary Queen of Scots

took refuge when she fled to England in 1568 after her defeat at Langside.' This section of the route was the province of the Cockermouth & Workington Railway, opened in 1847 initially to provide a link for the export of coal from the lower Derwent Valley via the port of Workington. It was one of the first railways in West Cumberland to be taken over by the LNWR, which operated the lines from Carlisle, Maryport and down the coast to

Whitehaven, later to include the Moor Row and Cleator Moor area (see Tour 18, the Ennerdale Lake & Calder Abbey Tour, for more details of this region).

Workington's history dates from Roman times when it was the site of a Hadrianic fort that formed part of the Roman coastal defences. The first recorded shipments of coal from Workington were to Ireland in 1604, and by the early 1800s the expansion of trade and industry in the area had resulted in an influx of workers not only from the surrounding region, but also from Ireland and Wales. Shipping through the harbour was increasing and in the three adjacent shipyards business was booming. The railway came to the town in 1847, primarily to facilitate the movement of coal and iron ore, thus connecting Workington with Whitehaven and Maryport, then on to Carlisle. In the same year, the line to Cockermouth was also opened. The Earl of Lonsdale, lord of the manor of Workington, invested heavily to improve the harbour at the beginning of the 19th century, and a new dock, subsequently to be enlarged to become the Prince of Wales Dock, was constructed.

An extract from an 1896 Furness Railway Map

ARMATHWAITE The luxury 4-star Armathwaite Hall boasts 'the only spa destination in the Lake District'.

Workington Hall, Front

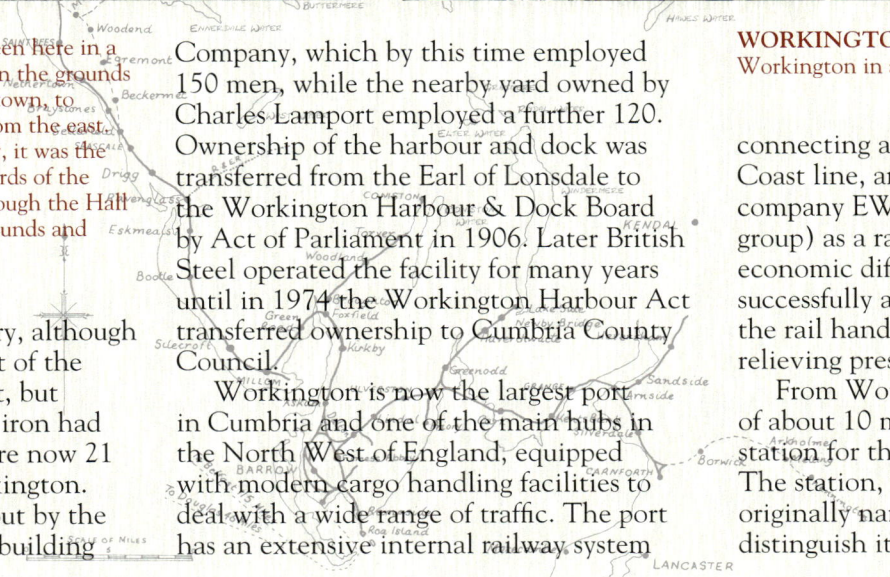

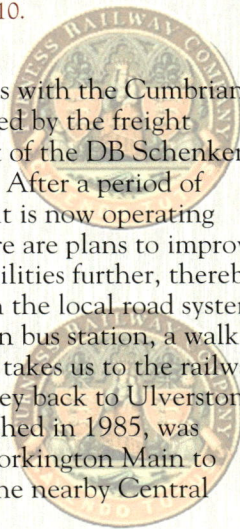

WORKINGTON Workington Hall, seen here in a postcard view from about 1909, stands in the grounds of Curwen Park on the outskirts of the town, to the right of the A66 as you approach from the east. Built as a piel tower in the 14th century, it was the hereditary seat of the Curwen family, lords of the manor of Workington until 1929. Although the Hall is currently closed to the public, the grounds and surrounding park are open to visitors.

By the end of the 19th century, although coal mining still continued, most of the smaller pits had been worked out, but the demand for Cumberland pig iron had increased so much that there were now 21 blast furnaces operating in Workington. Shipbuilding was being carried out by the Workington & Harrington Shipbuilding Company, which by this time employed 150 men, while the nearby yard owned by Charles Lamport employed a further 120. Ownership of the harbour and dock was transferred from the Earl of Lonsdale to the Workington Harbour & Dock Board by Act of Parliament in 1906. Later British Steel operated the facility for many years until in 1974 the Workington Harbour Act transferred ownership to Cumbria County Council.

Workington is now the largest port in Cumbria and one of the main hubs in the North West of England, equipped with modern cargo handling facilities to deal with a wide range of traffic. The port has an extensive internal railway system

WORKINGTON A postcard view of the harbour at Workington in about 1910.

connecting all berths with the Cumbrian Coast line, and is used by the freight company EWS (part of the DB Schenker group) as a railhead. After a period of economic difficulty it is now operating successfully and there are plans to improve the rail handling facilities further, thereby relieving pressure on the local road system.

From Workington bus station, a walk of about 10 minutes takes us to the railway station for the journey back to Ulverston. The station, refurbished in 1985, was originally named Workington Main to distinguish it from the nearby Central

WORKINGTON
Movement of goods through Workington's harbour and docks was in the care of shunters such as this 0-4-0ST No 19, built by the Yorkshire Engine Company of Sheffield as works number 2587 in 1954. It is seen here in about 1969.

WORKINGTON Another Yorkshire Engine Company 0-4-0ST, works number 2429, and behind it a Peckett & Sons Ltd 0-4-0ST languish at the Workington Haematite Iron Company in April 1966. Known as Workington Steel Works, established in 1856, it made pig iron from locally mined ore. Corus Rail operated the site, making rails, until its closure in 2006. The Indian engineering company Tata continues to operate in the town.

SIDDICK This Yorkshire Engine Company 0-4-0ST is works number 2431 of 1948, as is named NCB *St Helens No 2*. St Helens Colliery at Siddick, north of Workington, opened in 1880 and continued to produce coal into the National Coal Board era, finally being closed in 1966.

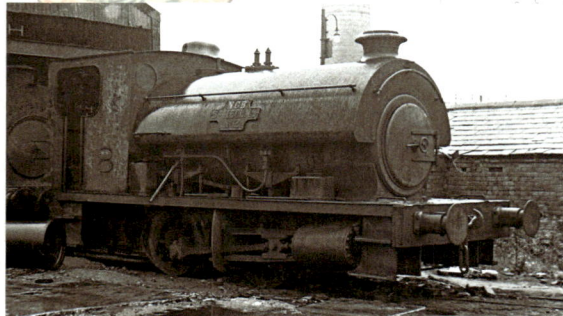

station of the Cleator & Workington Junction Railway (C&WJR), of which little remains today. The last part in operation was the branch to Linefoot for the Royal Navy Armaments Depot at Broughton Moor. This depot, decommissioned in 1992 at the end of the Cold War, was used by the United States Navy for storage of armaments for its North Atlantic Squadron. It had its own 2ft 6in (762mm) gauge railway, the locomotives from which are preserved on the Almond Valley Railway (Livingstone, Scotland) and Whipsnade Railway (Dunstable, Bedfordshire). The branch connecting the depot to the main line was also closed in 1992.

The Cumbrian Coast line runs from Carlisle to Barrow-in-Furness, so be aware that some services over this line require a change of train at Barrow in order to complete the journey to Ulverston. Workington Docks can be seen to the west as we travel the route of the former Whitehaven Junction Railway, absorbed into the LNWR in 1866. Across the Solway Firth are the first peaks of Scotland, with the highest visible being Criffel in southern Galloway, which at 1,870 feet (570 metres) dominates the coastal landscape.

Travelling south towards **Whitehaven** we skirt the Irish Sea, where the Isle of Man is visible on clear days. This coal-mining area was once dotted with collieries served by extensive rail links long since disappeared. The stretch of sea wall on the approach to the town is known locally as 'Avalanche Alley' as a result of the slippages from the nearby colliery tip, which block the line from time to time necessitating the provision of temporary bus services.

Whitehaven's railway pedigree dates back to 1735, when a short horse and gravity operated wooden wagonway was opened on the south side of the town to carry coal to the

An extract from an 1896 Furness Railway Map

harbour. The wagons were lowered to the harbour by means of a rope-worked incline known as the Howgill Brake. Much later, in 1881, a second such incline called the Corkickle Brake was constructed to connect Ladysmith Colliery to the Furness Railway's line, thereby enabling its coal to be more easily transported away. Ladysmith closed in 1931, but the Corkickle Brake found further employment with the expansion of the Marchon Products chemical company (purchased by Albright & Wilson Ltd in 1955), which took over the coking plant site in 1943 and made use of the system until 1986,

when a major redevelopment and restructuring of the site was undertaken, coincidentally in the year in which Haig Colliery, Whitehaven's last operational pit, finally closed.

Much of Haig Colliery's coal was mined beneath the sea but, after reaching the surface at cliff-top level, it had to be transported downhill again to the coal sidings at Whitehaven Docks.

WHITEHAVEN NCB No 6, an Andrew Barclay 0-4-0ST, works at Whitehaven's Haig Colliery in the 1970s. A fleet of industrial steam locos was responsible for handling the output of the more than 70 pits in the district, with much of it being transported to Whitehaven harbour for export by sea, primarily to Ireland.

WHITEHAVEN It's the end of the line for these locos, awaiting their final journeys from the scrap-line at Ladysmith Colliery, Whitehaven, in 1972. The first picture shows an 0-4-0ST by the Yorkshire Engine Company Ltd of Sheffield, the second another 0-4-0 saddle tank by Andrew Barclay, Sons & Co Ltd of Kilmarnock. Although the mine closed in 1931, the coal washery continued in use by nearby Haig Colliery, the last in the Cumberland coalfield, which itself ceased production in 1984. However, the winding gear and adjacent winding house still survive as part of the Haig Colliery Museum (see www.visitcumbria.com/wc/haig-colliery-mining-museum).

The colliery incline was far too steep for normal adhesion working, hence the adoption of rope-haulage to lower coal wagons to the harbour.

The cliff-top railway system at Haig was connected to the siding from the engine shed by a steep incline and what was described by Steven Oakden in an article for *Steam Railway* magazine in March 1985 as an 'atrocious single line track standing high on the cliffs above Whitehaven and looking out towards the Solway Firth'. The line ran down this steep incline through fields and past a few rows of miners' cottages, 'being dead straight (if you ignored the contortion of the rails themselves)'. Haig yard, according to Oakden,

Below: **LOWCA COLLIERY** Industrial steam works at the Lowca Colliery, 2 miles north of Whitehaven. The colliery was connected to Workington by the Lowca Light Railway, opened in 1913. Trains were operated by the Cleator & Workington Junction Railway and the line boasted the steepest gradient in Britain to carry adhesion-worked passenger trains – a short 285-yard (257-metre) stretch at 1 in 17. Lowca Colliery ceased winding in 1968, but the coal preparation plant was retained to wash the output from Solway Colliery at Workington. National Coal Board locos took charge of these deliveries from the exchange sidings of the former Whitehaven, Cleator & Egremont Railway's line. This picture, taken in September 1972, features on the right Vulcan Foundry 0-6-0ST *Amazon*, works number 5291 built in 1945, with Hunslet 0-6-0ST *Warspite*, works number 3778, built in 1952 to the same design, on the left. The latter is clearly identifiable due to its coal bunker 'extension', fitted in response to the passing of the Clean Air Acts of 1956 as part of an experiment to reduce black smoke by burning a mixture of coal and coke, which needed to be kept separate. The experiment proved unsuccessful and was soon abandoned.

'resembled a battlefield more than anything else. Derailed and condemned wagons stood where they had left the track, some upright, some on their sides. The sidings were buried up to rail-top level in coal dust. Subsidence, causing a large dip in the yard which ran across all the sidings, added to the general scene of ramshackle abandon.' As the line entered the large yard at Haig it went through a reverse curve, 'the scene and cause of much trouble', then ran dead straight to a head-shunt at the bottom of the yard. Here, one of several locos, the 0-6-0ST *Respite*, was to finish her days at Haig after running away down the track. She was subsequently sent to Walkden

Workshops, Manchester, for overhaul and repair, later to be relocated to Bickershaw Colliery at Leigh, Lancashire, where she worked as the last steam engine in use until the pit was 'dieselised' in March 1979. The next year she was donated by the National Coal Board to the Science Museum. Haig Colliery now enjoys a new lease of life as the Haig Mining Museum, which can be visited by taking the B5345 road south towards St Bees.

Once acknowledged as the most important sea port in Cumberland, it has been observed that, as applied to the present 'haven', the epithet 'white' was a huge misnomer, the principal export being

coal. This once important coal-mining area is now noted for its 'wind farm' of seven turbines sited on the cliffs above the Irish Sea at a height of 50 metres, offering a change of emphasis towards more modern 'green' energy production.

Whitehaven has seen considerable investment and rejuvenation in recent years, initially due to millennium developments and later in connection with the town's 300th anniversary celebrations. These included the refurbished 'Beacon', a museum set in the harbour and opened by HM the Queen and Prince Philip in 2008. The harbour lost its last commercial cargo handling operations in 1992 with

WHITEHAVEN
Whitehaven Bransty station was once the terminus of the Furness Railway. The station boasts a 1,322-yard-long tunnel under the town, with Bransty signal box at its northern end.

An extract from an 1896 Furness Railway Map

the ending of mineral traffic, and today the major industry is in connection with the British Nuclear Fuels complex at nearby Sellafield. The town's extremely popular Maritime Festival, held annually in June, includes such attractions as 'tall ships', air displays, street entertainers and firework displays.

The town marks the northern extent of the Furness Railway and still boasts two railway stations, Whitehaven (known as Whitehaven Bransty until 1968, rebuilt in 1981 and sometimes known as 'the new station'), and Corkickle, reached after passing under the town centre by means of Bransty Tunnel.

About 8 miles (13km) to the east of Whitehaven is the village of Ennerdale Bridge and the charming valley of Ennerdale Water. Once part of the ancient royal manor and forest of Copeland, it is completely enclosed by lofty hills and eloquently described in poems such as 'The Brothers' by Wordsworth.

The railway next passes close to the once thriving network of lines around Moor Row on our left (see Tour 18), also providing fine views of the Lakeland Fells beyond. We soon reach **St Bees**, which according to Bradshaw is 'so called from St Bega, an Irish saint who founded a monastery at this place in 650 AD'. The

Furness Railway Class 'D4' 0-6-0 goods engine No 4 is portrayed on a Raphael Tuck & Sons Ltd postcard produced for the Furness Railway in the 'FR Rolling Stock (The Present)' Series No 19, circa 1910. The 'D4s' were introduced by Pettigrew as a mixed-traffic version of his successful 'D3' mineral engines. Only four were built, FR Nos 3-6, entering service in 1907. Two were stationed at Whitehaven and the other two at Carnforth for fast goods work and also for occasional use on passenger services, for which they were fitted with vacuum brakes and steam heating equipment. Nos 3, 5 and 6 were rebuilt in 1926 with Lancashire & Yorkshire Railway boilers and extended smokeboxes. No 4 remained as built and was withdrawn in 1930, together with Nos 3 and 6. No 5 remained in service until 1934. They were renumbered 12480-83 by the LMS in the same order as their FR numbers.

coast here rises to the dramatic heights of the only major sea cliffs between Wales and Scotland and the only Heritage Coastline in Cumbria, being designated a Site of Special Scientific Interest (SSSI). The facilities at Seacote Park on South Head include extensive parking with toilets and showers. The nearby St Bees Head RSPB Reserve is home to the largest seabird colony in north-west England, while the village itself is the starting point for the 190-mile (304km) Coast to Coast Walk across northern England to Robin Hood's Bay on the North Yorkshire coast. The nearby lighthouse to the west was erected in 1822.

ST. BEES HEAD.
ST. BEES STATION.

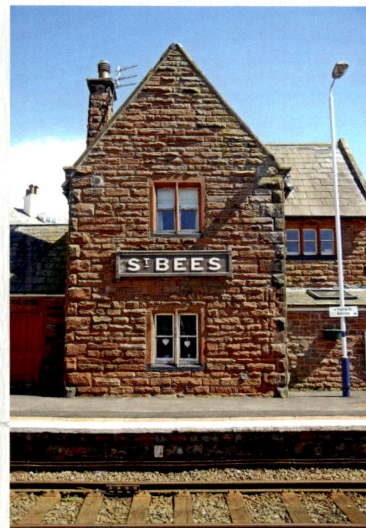

Above left: **ST BEES HEAD** The sea cliffs at St Bees Head are shown on a postcard produced for the Furness Railway by Raphael Tuck, Series 8, circa 1910.

Left: **ST BEES** The station and signal box.

Above left and right: **ST BEES** The buildings on the southbound platform have been converted to house 'Lu-Lu's Bistro & Wine Bar', decorated with railway memorabilia and offering accommodation and an appetising international menu. For further information, visit www.lulusbistro.co.uk. Thanks to the owner, Lou Morland, for her kind permission to photograph the premises.

Continuing along the line as it clings to the Irish Sea coast, we pass **Sellafield**, where the line from the nuclear plant joins from the left. A triangle was installed here in 1982 for turning steam locomotives heading

rail tours along this lovely Cumbrian Coast route from Carnforth, but the facility has recently been withdrawn following concerns over safety and security. Passing the lovely beaches of **Seascale** we come to **Drigg**, with its

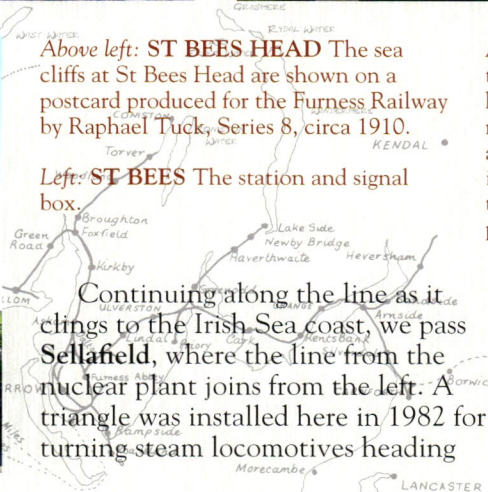

sidings serving the low-level radioactive waste depository, then to the only coastal village in the Lake District National Park, **Ravenglass**, 16½ miles (26km) from Whitehaven and situated where the rivers Esk and Mite pour into the sea.

Ravenglass is the home of the narrow-gauge Ravenglass & Eskdale Railway, which was originally built to a 3-foot (900mm) gauge purely as a freight-carrying line to facilitate the transport of iron ore from the head of the Esk Valley at the remote Nab Gill, some 9 miles (14km) from civilisation and previously reliant on horse and cart. The destination was an exchange wharf with the Furness Railway on the eastern side of Ravenglass goods yard consisting of two dead-end sidings, a small two-road engine shed and a workshop. One of the sidings ran parallel to an FR goods siding, from where the iron ore could be discharged into that company's standard-gauge wagons to then join the

main line. The route from Ravenglass, laid in 1875, followed the River Mite alongside Muncaster Fell before entering Eskdale at Eskdale Green, the only sizeable community along the route, and the location of the line's smithy. The railway then ran on up the dale on varying grades before a last hard climb of about half a mile at up to 1 in 34 to the foot of the Nab Gill incline, where there was a scattering of houses referred to at the time as 'the Boot', now just Boot, where a run-round loop was provided.

The railway immediately proved its worth with large volumes of iron ore and limestone being carried down to Ravenglass, and there was soon pressure

Left: **ST BEES** The statue of St Bega, opposite the station.

Right: **ST BEES** The beach at South Head.

An extract from an 1896 Furness Railway Map

FURNESS RAILWAY,
Wastwater Circular Tour
Avl as per Advertisement

Whitehaven
TO
RAVENGLASS
& BACK

First Class

NonTransferable

FURNESS RAILWAY,
Wastwater Circular Tour
Rail & Coach

Ravenglass
TO
DALEGARTH
via N.G.Ry & MOTOR
& BACK To
RAVENGLASS
Avl as per Advertisement
See Over

Never slow to spot an opportunity, the FR joined forces with the narrow-gauge Ravenglass & Eskdale Railway to promote this tour.

from local inhabitants to introduce a passenger service. However, the Board of Trade Inspector sent to examine the line in June 1876, one Colonel Yolland, issued a scathing report, stating that the line was in no shape to accommodate passenger services, citing inadequate clearances, indifferent construction quality, incomplete stations and only one locomotive. Something had to be done, and it was done promptly! Raised platforms with waiting huts were constructed and a second locomotive acquired. Other improvements to the construction of the line went ahead and a further inspection by Colonel Yolland was carried out in November of that same year, after which he was sufficiently appeased to give his cautious

blessing, whereupon passenger services were introduced to a regular timetable. Thus began the chequered history of the Ravenglass & Eskdale Railway.

In time the Nab Gill lodes became increasingly difficult to work. The price of iron ore fell and the railway soon ran into financial difficulties, leading to its closure in 1913. It later reopened when granite quarrying provided a source of revenue, with some passenger trains operating, though this again failed to be commercially viable and the line was again closed down and put up for sale by auction in 1960. Eventually in the 1960s, after a period

of dereliction, the Ravenglass & Eskdale Railway Preservation Society was formed by enthusiasts who outbid the scrap dealers to save the day. Finally the 7-mile stretch, now converted to a 15-inch (381mm) gauge and known affectionately as the 'La'al Ratty', was in business again.

In recent years extensive refurbishment of track, equipment, rolling stock and locomotives, as well as improved facilities for visitors, has transformed the ailing freight line into a successful tourist attraction. A conversion of the old BR station building at Ravenglass has become its own pub, The Ratty Arms, welcoming the visitors who flock from all over the world to enjoy the unspoilt nature of Eskdale.

The line up the Esk Valley, described by Wainwright as 'one of the loveliest

ESKDALE Dalegarth Hall, Eskdale, reproduced from *Walking in the Lake District* by H. H. Symonds, published by Alexander Maclehose & Co in 1933. The ancient manor house, built in 1599, is now a Grade II listed building.

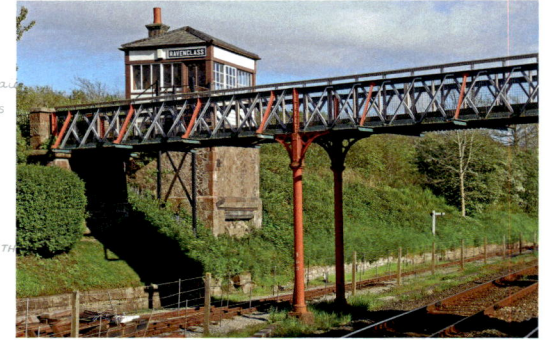

RAVENGLASS At Ravenglass station on the Cumbrian Coast line, Class 153 DMU No 153304 heads for Carlisle. The station buildings now house The Ratty Arms pub – 'real ale, real food and real music'.

Right: **RAVENGLASS** The footbridge and signal box.

of Lakeland's valleys', is impressive, with a maximum gradient of 1 in 55 to test the little steam locomotives as they haul their trains up to the terminus at Dalegarth for Boot station, at the foot of England's highest and wildest mountains, the Scafell range. Wainwright commented that, from the summit of Scafell Pike, 'on a clear day you can see the five Kingdoms – Scotland, Ireland, Wales, the Isle of Man, and Heaven!' Scafell Pike is also famed as one of the three British peaks climbed as part

Left: **RAVENGLASS** The 'La'al Ratty' station with a platform canopy from Millom station still bearing its FR insignia.

Right: **HARD KNOTT PASS** The route over the rugged landscape of Hard Knott Pass follows fairly closely the route of the Roman road from the fort at Ambleside, through Eskdale and on to the port of Ravenglass. Sitting on an outcrop in the steep hillside overlooking Eskdale are the remains of Mediobogdum, a Roman fort perfectly situated to control movement across this strategic point. The second view shows a more benign aspect, looking down the Pass towards Eskdale.

Left: **DALEGARTH** At Dalegarth for Boot station (often simply referred to as 'Dalegarth', though it was originally 'Eskdale (Dalegarth)', 2-8-2 No 7 *River Esk* is turned ready to take the return train to Ravenglass at Easter 1977. The loco was built in 1923 by Davey, Paxman & Co of Colchester (later manufacturers of diesel engines powering such as the BR Class 43 HSTs and the Class 56 and 58 locomotives). No 7 has been on the 'La'al Ratty' since 1923 and is currently undergoing overhaul.

Left: **ESK VALLEY** *River Esk* heads back down the Esk Valley once more. Since these photographs were taken a new station and visitor centre has been built at Dalegarth, opened in 2007 by Pete Waterman.

of the National Three Peaks Challenge, the others being Ben Nevis (the highest mountain in Scotland), and Snowdon (the highest in Wales).

Close by Ravenglass is the privately owned Muncaster Castle, with its beautiful grounds and gardens. In medieval times it was a fortified tower, and is now open daily from February through to December (though often closed to the public on Saturdays for private functions). The Grade I listed building also boasts an owl sanctuary, a maze, attractive Himalayan Gardens and, reportedly, a resident ghost!

Continuing our journey south our train passes over Eskmeals Viaduct to the site of

An extract from an 1896 Furness Railway Map

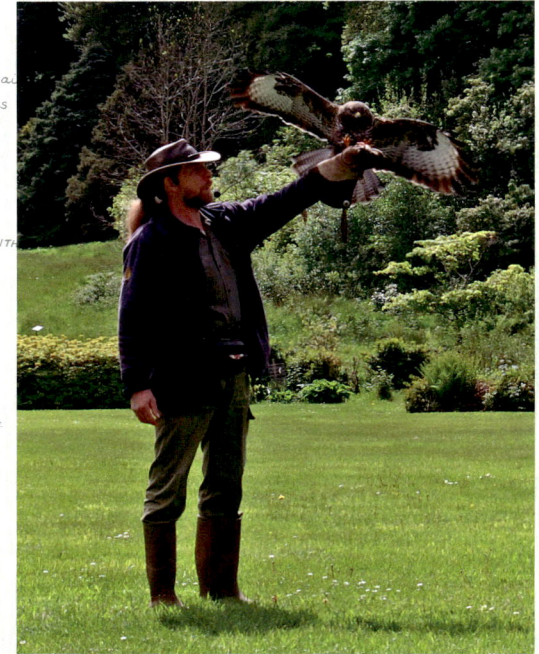

MUNCASTER CASTLE houses the World Owl Centre, home to one of the finest collections in the world, currently numbering 50 species together with other raptors including the common buzzard and red kite. With an emphasis on the increasing need for conservation in light of the continuing threat to owl populations worldwide, the Centre's programme of reintroducing birds into the wild is having increasing success. Centre staff promote their cause by means of regular 'meet the birds' events, where visitors learn more of the valuable work carried out at there.

Left and above: **MUNCASTER CASTLE** A common buzzard demonstrates its agility, while a European eagle owl eyes the audience.

Eskmeals station, closed to passengers in 1959, although the disused platforms still remain. Very little evidence remains of the once extensive rail system associated with the iron workings in this area, or of the nearby sidings that served the Vickers Gun Range. Today the Eskmeals Firing Range continues to operate as a Ministry of Defence Weapons Research Establishment,

specialising in range and accuracy trials. It is now accessible only by road from the ancient market town of **Bootle**, whose station is now a 'request stop'. The local hill known as Black Combe is well worth the hour and a half's easy climb offering a spectacular panorama of blue-topped hills, lovely dales, towns, rivers, woods and islands, which is said to encompass no fewer than 14 counties of England and Scotland.

We continue to the small town of **Millom**, which owes its existence to the discovery of iron ore at nearby Hodbarrow,

south of the town, in 1855, following which the population of the small village expanded to more than 10,000. The Hodbarrow mine was one of the most successful iron ore mines in Cumberland (now Cumbria), not only for the amount that was excavated, but also for the quality of the haematite. The Hodbarrow Mining Company did, however, suffer early setbacks due to seawater seepage causing the workings to collapse, but perseverance brought its rewards when in 1868 extra boreholes were sunk and a huge amount

Below: **MILLOM** Kerr Stuart 0-4-0ST No 11 of 1919, works number 4009, poses at the Millom Haematite Ore & Iron Company (Millom Ironworks) on 9 June 1962. The company operated a small fleet of these saddle tank locos, and stablemate No 1 (works number AB 2333) was among the lucky ones rescued for preservation, transferring to Carnforth Steamtown upon closure of the works. There it was nicknamed 'David', and was later resold and transferred in 1978 to the Lakeside & Haverthwaite Railway, where it is still working today.

Right: **MILLOM** This was the scene at the Hodbarrow mine in 1962, with 0-4-0 Crane Tank No 6, built by Neilson & Co of Glasgow in 1890, works number N 4004. These crane tanks were frequently used in industrial locations such as docks, mines and railway works, where they could operate as both shunter and mobile crane. 'Snipey', seen here, was used to carry pit trucks and props at the Millom & Hodbarrow Haematite Ore and Iron Company's works.

of haematite was discovered. Though the problems with flooding continued, the highly valued ore was incentive enough for major schemes to be undertaken with the aim of keeping the mine free of seawater. The most successful sea defence was built in the early 1900s and is still in good condition today, even though the mine ceased production in 1967 after 112 years. Millom Ironworks closed its doors for the final time in 1968, and the site has been developed into a Local Nature Reserve beside the Duddon Estuary with the now deliberately flooded Hodbarrow mining site having become a major RSPB bird reserve.

Millom station, opened by the Whitehaven & Furness Junction Railway in 1850, is now managed by Northern Rail, with hourly services operating in both directions (except Sundays). The station buildings are home to the Millom Heritage Museum and Visitor Centre, which also runs the rail ticket office. Millom Castle, for several centuries the seat of the powerful Lords of Millom, is about a mile from the station along the A595 Broughton road; although of historical interest, it is seldom open to the public.

The railway now makes a long detour around **Duddon Sands**, the wide estuary

An extract from an 1896 Furness Railway Map

of the River Duddon where it empties into the Irish Sea after its journey from the heights of the Wrynose Pass. Before local government reorganisation in 1974, the River Duddon formed the boundary between the historic counties of Lancashire and Cumberland. The Sands provide a rich source of shellfish for the markets of Liverpool, Fleetwood and Whitehaven. At nearly 3 miles (5km) across, they are notoriously treacherous in places and are

the site of numerous fatal accidents caused by the rapidity with which the tide flows in. The Duddon Estuary is designated as a Site of Special Scientific Interest and, with Hodbarrow RSPB reserve, forms an extensive area of brackish water and golden sands, rich with invertebrates.

Travelling onward we pass over the impressive Duddon Viaduct, 396 yards (356m) long with 49 spans, to arrive at Foxfield, then on to the one-time terminus

Above left and top: **MILLOM** Class 153 DMU No 153324 gathers passengers at Millom for the journey towards Carlisle on 14 May 2014. The station today bears little resemblance to that of steam's glory years – gone are the turntable and extensive sidings, but the signal box is still standing.

Above: **MILLOM** The Lancaster-bound platform canopy at Millom station proudly shows its FR origins. The corresponding canopy from the Carlisle platform now shelters visitors to the Ravenglass & Eskdale Railway at Ravenglass station.

An extract from an 1896 Furness Railway Map

MILLOM Double-headed DRS Class 37s Nos 37608 and 37607 head the Sellafield (BNF) to Crewe Coal Sidings low-level radioactive waste train, which runs through Millom on most days.

of the Whitehaven & Furness Junction Railway at **Broughton in Furness**. Ulpha to the north and the Vale of Duddon are the subjects of some of Wordsworth's finest poetry, while the Druidical Temple at Swineside, 3-4 miles (about 6km) west of Broughton, is reputed to be one of the most perfect in the North of England.

In the 1850s a Furness Railway coach would connect with the train at Broughton and proceed daily to and from Coniston, Hawkshead, Ambleside and the Kendal & Windermere Railway. The distance from Broughton to Coniston Waterhead is 10 miles (16km), and from there the neighbouring vales of Tilberthwaite, Yewdale and Langdale can be easily explored, the latter of course offering the ascent of the 'Old Man'.

Turning south we head for at the large town, seaport and one-time headquarters of the Furness Railway, Barrow-in-Furness – see Tour 1, the Outer Circular Tour (page 99), for further details of this area.

Passing the former monastery of Furness Abbey, which dates from 1123, we come to the end of our Five Lakes Circular Tour, back at Ulverston railway station.

For those opting to take the alternative return route from Keswick by way of Penrith and the West Coast Main Line, the X4 or X5 bus service to Penrith railway station runs hourly from Keswick bus station and the journey takes about 45 minutes. The journey east along the A66 retraces parts of the line of the Cockermouth, Keswick & Penrith Railway. Keswick station now marks the start of a spectacular 2-mile (3.2km) railway

footpath through the Greta Gorge, which includes a tunnel and eight girder bridges, purchased with the trackbed between Keswick and Threlkeld in 1983 by the Lake District National Park Authority. The intermediate stations en route to Penrith were Low Brierly, Threlkeld, Highgate, Troutbeck, Penruddock and Blencow.

The site of the former **Threlkeld** Quarry has now become the Threlkeld Quarry & Mining Museum. Opened in the 1870s to supply ballast for the Penrith

An extract from an 1896 Furness Railway Map

THRELKELD QUARRY & MINING MUSEUM is home to possibly the largest collection of 'steam navvies' in the world, including the impressive 'King Kong', aka Ruston Bucyrus 110 RB No 7.

MILLOM CASTLE stands about a mile from the town along the A595 towards Broughton in Furness. Look out on the left-hand side for wooden signs to Holy Trinity Church, Castle & The Old School Room tea room. The castle is not generally open to the public – only infrequently during the year on special occasions.

to Keswick railway, it later provided stone for the Manchester Corporation Waterworks for its Thirlmere scheme, ballast for the West Coast Main Line, and roadstone, kerbing and dressed stone for other projects. The quarry was eventually closed in 1982, and in the 1990s the site

was acquired by the Lakeland Mines & Quarries Trust, whose members set about restoring the quarry and developing it into the amenity it is today – an attraction with a unique collection of machinery and offering underground tours (prior booking required) as well as the opportunity to pan for minerals. There is also a narrow-gauge railway operated by the company's restored steam locomotives. To see the museum's

Left: **THRELKELD QUARRY AND MINING MUSEUM** The mine entrance.

Right: **THRELKELD QUARRY AND MINING MUSEUM** 0-4-0ST *Askham Hall*, works number 1772, was built by the Avonside Engine Company of Bristol in 1917 and is one of several exhibits awaiting restoration. Thanks to quarry-owner Ian Hartland for his kind welcome and permission to use images of the site.

publicity materials and opening times, visit www. threlkeldquarryandminingmuseum.co.uk.

At Penrith railway station, trains run regularly south over the high-speed West Coast Main Line, over the famous Shap summit, considered quite a challenge in steam days, especially from the south, then on through Tebay and Carnforth (where unfortunately they no longer stop) to Lancaster. Here we must change to the Barrow-in-Furness service for the final leg of the journey back to Ulverston.

TROUT BECK VALLEY In the valley of the Trout Beck, between Keswick and Penrith, conditions are harsh in winter.

TROUTBECK The remains of the CK&PR's Troutbeck station and signal box on 30 December 1979.

Map of Tour No 18 (2015)

Route by bus + + +
Route by rail —

Whitehaven
Cleator Moor
Moor Row
St Bees
Egremont
Nethertown
Calder Bridge
Braystones
Sellafield
Gosforth
Seascale

Irish Sea

Tour 18: The Ennerdale Lake and Calder Abbey Tour (modified)

Seascale-Gosforth-Calder Bridge-Egremont-Moor Row-Cleator Moor (optional)-Whitehaven-Seascale

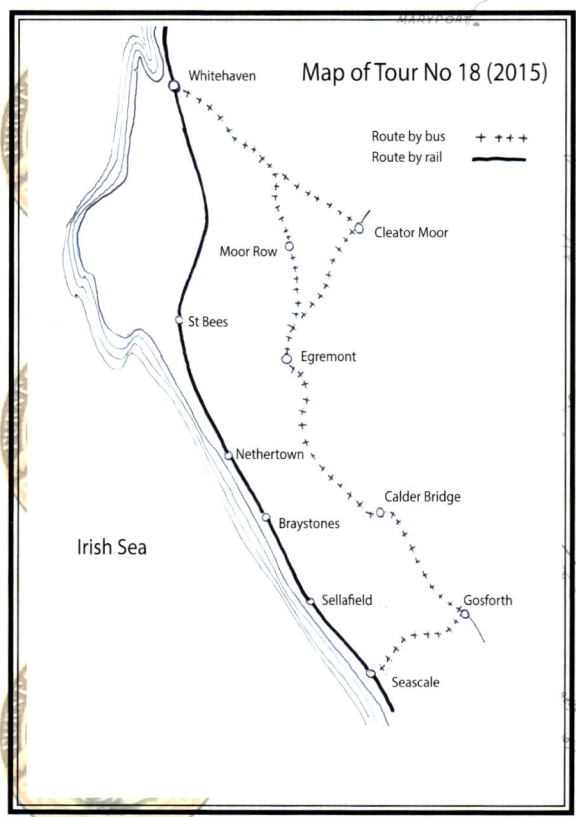

By bus from Seascale to Moor Row – bus to Whitehaven (via Cleator Moor – optional) – national rail to Seascale

- Allow about 6½ hours for the full itinerary
- Suggested starting point: Seascale, outside St Cuthbert's Church

This circular tour has fascinating early railway interest centred around the Moor Row-Cleator-Rowrah area to the east of Whitehaven, as well as the opportunity to visit Calder Abbey and to travel on the delightful Cumbrian Coast line.

The tour begins on the western fringe of the Lake District on the Irish Sea coast at **Seascale**, easily reached by means of the former Furness Railway line from Carnforth and Barrow-in-Furness. The line here was built by the Whitehaven & Furness Junction Railway and skirted the coast for 35 miles (56km) as far south as Broughton in Furness, where it joined the Furness Railway's line to the ports of Piel and Barrow, about 15 miles (24km) away. In fact, Seascale's popularity as a seaside resort is due in no small measure to the accessibility that resulted from the coming of the railway in 1850. Being rich in history and boasting miles of clean sandy beaches, Seascale has established itself as an ideal centre from which to explore the western Lake District.

One minute from the railway station is St Cuthbert's Church, where we,

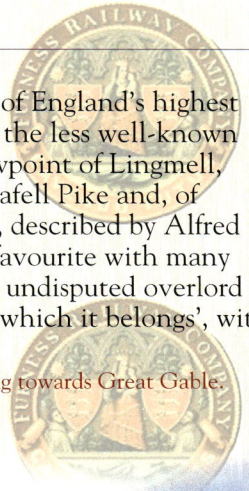

Tour 18: Suggested route and connections

By bus (6 or X6)
dep Seascale 9.59 or 11.59 via Egremont to Moor Row (Church St, outside the Post Office) (approx 35 mins)
By bus (6)
dep Moor Row (Church St) to Whitehaven railway station (approx 20 mins)

To visit Cleator Moor from Moor Row, return by bus 6 from Moor Row to Egremont (approx 10 mins), then take bus 22 from Egremont Main St (outside No 77) to Cleator Moor (High St, at Square) (approx 15 mins). From Cleator Moor to Whitehaven station, take bus 22, 31 or 32 to Whitehaven (Lowther St) (approx 20 mins), then 10-minute walk past Inner Harbour and Dock to railway station

By rail
Whitehaven to Seascale

Note: Bus, rail and ferry timetables can change at very short notice. Be sure to check details before travelling.

for example, board the 9.59 service 6 bus towards Whitehaven. This takes us a mile or two inland to the edge of the fells, where we pick up the main coastal road, the A595, at **Gosforth**, described as an exceptionally beautiful village backed by 'the most breathtaking and untouched scenery in England'. Amid this glory, at the head of the nearby Wasdale Valley lies England's deepest lake, Wast Water,

surrounded by some of England's highest mountains. There is the less well-known but magnificent viewpoint of Lingmell, as well as Scafell, Scafell Pike and, of course, Great Gable, described by Alfred Wainwright as first favourite with many fell-walkers and 'the undisputed overlord of the group of hills to which it belongs', with

WAST WATER looking towards Great Gable.

the view from the top being claimed as the finest in the Lake District.

Less than 15 minutes into our journey we arrive at **Calder Bridge**. An option is to disembark here to explore the village and its surroundings, then take the next bus to Moor Row, which is due along at about 11.50. The village contains two inns dating from the 19th century, one of which, the Golden Fleece, was once hosted by a landlord who for many years was acknowledged as the undisputed champion of the English Wrestling Ring. The other inn, the Stanley's Arms, has a romantic garden overlooking the River Calder.

About a mile (1.6km) away, the ruins of the monastery of **Calder Abbey**, founded in 1134 and described as 'one of the most enchanting in the British Isles' are privately owned and unfortunately not regularly open to the public. The Abbey was once home to a brotherhood of 12 Cistercian monks from Furness Abbey, but unfortunately after only five years it was attacked and despoiled by an army of Scots and Glaswegians under King David I of Scotland. The fleeing monks were then refused re-entry to Furness Abbey and went instead to York, where the Archbishop took them in for a time before they went on to found Byland Abbey in 1142. Calder Abbey was soon reoccupied by a second colony from Furness, who dwelt there until its dissolution in 1536.

The village of Calder Bridge has other treasures to explore. Three splendid houses, Calder Abbey House, Pelham House (first known as Ponsonby

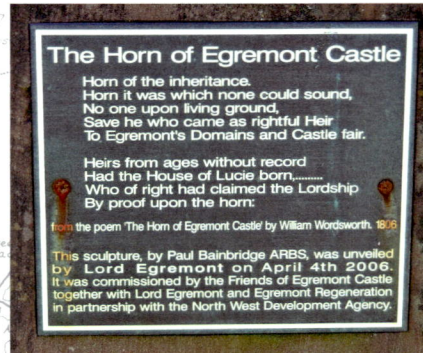

The Horn of Egremont Castle

Horn of the inheritance.
Horn it was which none could sound,
No one upon living ground,
Save he who came as rightful Heir
To Egremont's Domains and Castle fair.

Heirs from ages without record
Had the House of Lucie born,..........
Who of right had claimed the Lordship
By proof upon the horn:

from the poem 'The Horn of Egremont Castle' by William Wordsworth. 1806

This sculpture, by Paul Bainbridge ARBS, was unveiled by **Lord Egremont on April 4th 2006.** It was commissioned by the Friends of Egremont Castle together with Lord Egremont and Egremont Regeneration in partnership with the North West Development Agency.

EGREMONT CASTLE (free entry) has a tree trail and sculpture depicting the Egremont Horn.

Hall) and Sella Park are elegant buildings in themselves, while the two churches, St Bridget's and the nearby Ponsonby Church, both boast rare Pre-Raphaelite stained glass. An ancient path from here to Cold Fell features the oldest packhorse bridge in Cumbria; still in use today, it was originally built for the monks of Calder Abbey, hence its name, Monks Bridge.

Continuing our tour, we pass through the market town of **Egremont**, described as 'a place of great antiquity'. It was once the capital of the great barony of Copeland and the place where the feudal lords had their headquarters. Its wide Main Street leads to the market place with the remains of a splendid Norman castle built in the 12th century. This and the church, with its unusual font, are both of considerable interest to the visitor. The town once had a railway station on the Whitehaven, Cleator & Egremont Railway (WC&ER), opened in 1855. Its lines ran inland from Mirehouse Junction, 1 mile (1.6km) south of Whitehaven, to Moor Row Junction, from where its northern

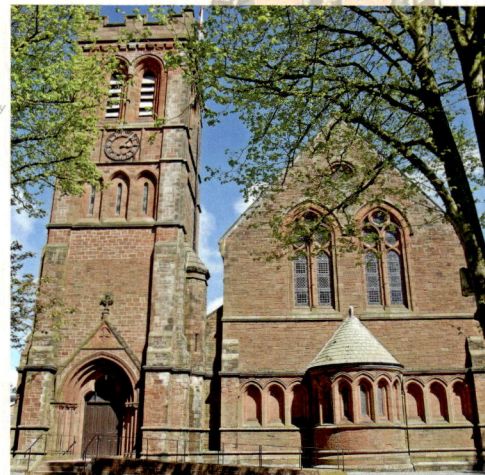

EGREMONT The imposing frontage of the church of St Mary & St Michael.

section led to Cleator Moor, Rowrah, Ullock and on to Marron Junction where it joined the London & North Western's metals (the LNWR had taken over the Cockermouth & Workington Railway in 1866). The southern section of the WC&ER went from Moor Row to Egremont, and closed in 1947. The company also had several important branch lines serving local industries.

Shortly after Egremont we arrive at the hub of the railways in the area, **Moor Row**. 'The row of houses on the moor' shot to 'boom town' status in the 19th century following the discovery of major iron ore deposits in the vicinity, the resultant mine becoming the largest in the Whitehaven and Furness districts. The railway shunting yards that followed brought further jobs and prosperity to the village, and soon Moor Row was western Cumbria's most important junction and goods yard, a position it retained until after the Second World War. The WC&ER was taken over and owned jointly by the LNWR and the Furness Railway from 1878 until the 'Grouping' of 1923, when it became part of the LMS. When road haulage began to expand the railways fell into decline. Moor Row loco shed, situated next to the station on the Rowrah branch of the former WC&ER, housed a variety of former L&YR locos in the 1950s, including 4Fs 0-6-0s Nos 44461 and 44549, 'Jinties' Nos 47337/390/525/604, and 3F 0-6-0s 52201/285/418/494/499/510. The shed was closed on 31 July 1954, and the railway itself was finally closed in 1980 when limestone quarrying at Rowrah ceased and there was little other mining in the area.

Today the route of the railway can be readily followed as it forms part of the Coast to Coast Cycleway, along which evidence of the area's transport heritage can still be found.

MOOR ROW Outside Moor Row engine shed, coded 12E, on 2 August 1953 are Pettigrew 0-6-0 locos Nos 52510 and 52509. Introduced in 1913 for the Furness Railway, No 52509, furthest from the camera, was allocated to Barrow shed (11B) until withdrawn from service on 31 December 1956 and cut up at BR's Horwich Works soon after. Sister loco No 52510 was transferred to Carnforth shed (11A), but withdrawn as the last of her class on 31 August 1957 and also cut up at Horwich the following year. William Frank Pettigrew was appointed to the post of Locomotive & Wagon Superintendent of the Furness Railway in 1896 upon the retirement of Mr R. Mason, who had held the post since 1850. His appointment coincided with that of Alfred Aslett as General Manager.

Pettigrew came from the London & South Western Railway and, like Aslett, brought a wealth of new ideas to the Furness. This was a time when many of the locomotives were reaching the end of their working lives, and Pettigrew designed new stock to replace them – the first time the company had designed its own engines, having previously relied on standard types from outside builders. With Pettigrew's new designs and Aslett's flair for business, the company was soon in a very strong position. Coincidentally, both Aslett and Pettigrew retired in the same year, 1918. By their efforts, the financial circumstances of the railway company, the town of Barrow and the tradespeople of the Furness region had been greatly improved.

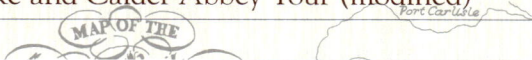

Left: **Nr WINDER** The Coast to Coast (C2C) Cycleway is seen near Winder, north-east of Cleator Moor. The route passes through Whitehaven, Moor Row and Cleator Moor, marked by mileposts showing directions, at the top of which are depictions of quarry carts used locally to transport iron ore and limestone.

Below left: **WINDER** The remains of Winder station in May 2014.

Below: **ROWRAH** At Rowrah, the Stork Hotel is the last public house and hotel in the village and, at 2 miles (3.2km) from Ennerdale Bridge on the C2C Cycleway, it was also the first stop for walkers on Wainwright's Coast to Coast Walk from St Bees to Robin Hood's Bay in North Yorkshire. The adjacent Railway Hotel, also known as the Station Hotel, was previously owned by Jennings Brewery of Cockermouth and, although now a private residence, it still displays elements of its railway origins.

Left: **CLEATOR MOOR** An ornate bridge over the trackbed at Cleator Moor.

Below: **Nr MOOR ROW** This viaduct near Moor Row stood on the former Cleator & Workington Junction Railway line from Moor Row to Siddick Junction, north of Workington. In the foreground is Keekle Community Park.

An extract from an 1896 Furness Railway Map

MOOR ROW Although Moor Row became western Cumbria's most important junction and goods yard, its decline was rapid after the Second World War, and the railway was closed in 1980 following the closure of the last mine in the area at Beckermet. Here we see the C2C Cycleway alongside the remains of Moor Row station.

From Moor Row it was a short journey by rail along the WC&ER to Cleator Moor, but if you decide to visit the town, as is so often the case, the bus service now takes a longer route, via Egremont. The town of **Cleator Moor** also expanded rapidly as a result of iron-ore mining in the area, but unlike Moor Row it suffered badly from subsidence, so much so that parts of the town had to be demolished and the railway line had to be rebuilt as a passenger deviation branch, leaving the original line from Moor Row to be used only by the iron ore trains. In addition to the WC&ER, Cleator Moor was also served by the Cleator & Workington

Left: FR Class 'L2' 0-6-2T No 104 is seen here at Grange station on an FR postcard from Raphael Tuck, circa 1910. Ten of these locos were built in 1904 and worked all over the system, though their main focus of operations was in the Cleator and Barrow districts. Intended originally as banking engines, their large wheels made them more suitable for passenger service so they were fitted with vacuum brakes and steam heating apparatus. No 104 was renumbered to 11631 by the LMS and withdrawn in 1930.

Above right and below: **ENNERDALE BRIDGE** The church of St Mary and The Fox & Hounds pub next to the river at Ennerdale Bridge.

Junction Railway, which had its own station on the western edge of the town, because of its importance in the industrial landscape of west Cumbria. Both companies passed into the ownership of the LMS in 1923, and unfortunately for the town that company had invested heavily in the local bus service, so to promote that interest it closed the railway to passengers in 1931.

From Cleator Moor, a short diversion of about 3 miles (5km) to the east takes us to the charming village of **Ennerdale Bridge**. Its quaint church, choice of two pubs nearby offering meals, and the lovely River Ehen flowing out of the secluded and peaceful Ennerdale Water on its doorstep, all combine to provide the traveller with the opportunity to take a welcome break.

Whether you have travelled by bus direct from Moor Row or via Cleator Moor, the final leg of the tour involves a rail journey from

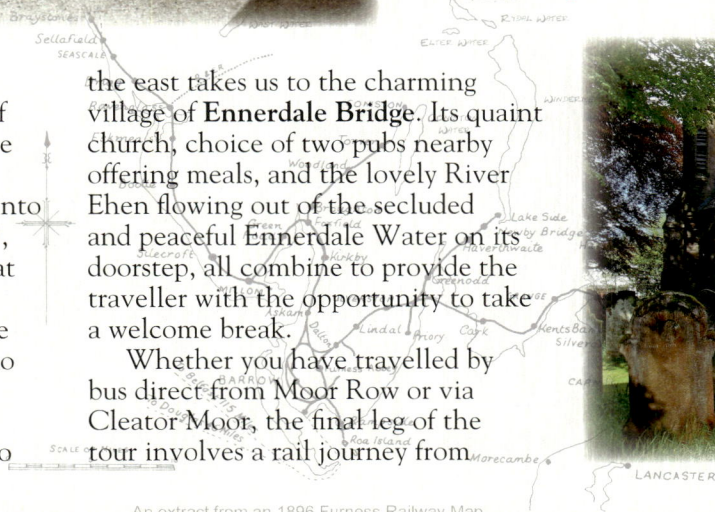

Whitehaven by means of the Northern Rail service, which takes us along the delightful Cumbrian Coast line back to our starting point at Seascale. In post-'Grouping' days, between 1923 and the end of steam traction in the 1960s, a variety of loco designs graced this very special route. Henry Fowler was Chief Mechanical Engineer (CME) with the Midland Railway and continued into LMS days, and his 4F 0-6-0 freight locos, introduced from 1911, were frequently to be seen as they were allocated to the sheds at Workington, Barrow and Carnforth, as well as Lancaster Green Ayre. There

Class 4P No 41113, a 4-4-0 three-cylinder 'Compound' built at Derby Works in November 1925, was allocated to Lancaster Green Ayre shed, so was frequently to be seen in the area until her withdrawal in 1958. She was later cut up at Cashmore's scrapyard at Great Bridge, Staffordshire.

they might have been seen alongside his passenger design, the 4P 4-4-0s, introduced from 1924. A total of 195 such locos were produced, adding to the 45 of the Midland Railway '1000' Class, to which they were almost identical. Of these, only the 'Midland Compound' No 1000 itself has survived into preservation.

Charles Fairburn succeeded the better-known William Stanier as CME of the LMS in 1944, and his 4F 2-6-4 tank locos were well known on Cumbrian lines. Several of the 280 members resided at Penrith, Barrow and Carnforth sheds. Other similar examples built by Fowler and Stanier brought the class total to 645, with Robert Riddles adding a further 155 BR

ENNERDALE An FR postcard view, circa 1902, *Ken Norman collection*

'Standard' examples in the 1950s, giving a grand total of 800 locos built over a period of about 30 years. A total of 15 of the BR variation have survived to adorn heritage railways up and down the country, making the design second only to the LMS Stanier 'Black 5' as the most preserved main-line class (with 18 examples saved). In addition, two of Fairburn's 4F tank engines can still be seen locally, as Nos 42073 and 42085 have found a home on the Lakeside & Haverthwaite Railway.

Visitors to west Cumbria in the summer months may be lucky enough to experience main-line steam in action over the Cumbrian Coast line. On certain Saturdays 'The Cumbrian Coast Express', a steam railtour organised by an independent tour operator, is hauled by a preserved express passenger locomotive, often a Stanier 'Jubilee' Class 4-6-0 of the former LMS, running between Carnforth and Carlisle by way of the Furness route.

For more information on the Cumbrian Coast line, refer to Tour 13, the Five Lakes Circular Tour (page 53).

Left: Fairburn 2-6-4T Nos 42085 with 42073 are under repair in Haverthwaite shed during April 2014.

Above: Preserved Stanier 'Jubilee' 4-6-0 No 5690 *Leander* has long been a favourite at the head of steam specials. *Douglas Todd*

An extract from an 1896 Furness Railway Map

Tour 19: Across the Ferry Tour

Bowness-Ferry Nab-Far Sawrey-Hawkshead-Esthwaite Water-Grizedale Forest-Tarn Hows-Hawkshead-Bowness

By bus and foot from Bowness to Ferry Nab – ferry to Ferry House – minibus to Hawkshead and return

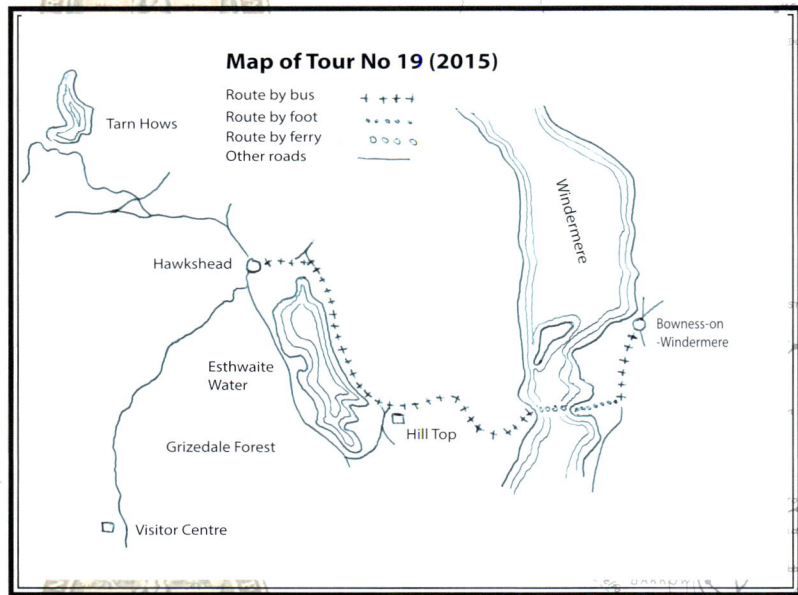

- Allow about 7½ hours for the full itinerary.
- Suggested starting point: Tourist Information Centre by the lake at Bowness-on-Windermere

Map of Tour No 19 (2015)

Route by bus
Route by foot
Route by ferry
Other roads

Tarn Hows

Hawkshead

Esthwaite Water

Grizedale Forest

Hill Top

Visitor Centre

Windermere

Bowness-on-Windermere

This delightful and varied day out begins at the Tourist Information Centre by the lake at Bowness-on-Windermere, about 10 minutes walk from the town centre. Refer to Tour 3 (page 19) for more details about Bowness. The bus number 6 in the direction of Newby Bridge for the short ride, a minute or two only, to the stop for the Windermere Ferry crossing at Ferry Nab by the Burnside Hotel. From here, a pleasant stroll brings us to the crossing. Originally rowed across the lake, later steam-driven and now powered by modern diesel engines, the Windermere Ferries have been carrying people, horses, cycles and vehicles between the busy eastern bank and the peaceful countryside to the west for more than 500 years. The service, operated by the Highways Department of Cumbria County Council, runs daily throughout the year (except Christmas Day and Boxing Day) between Ferry Nab and Ferry House, Far Sawrey, at 20-minute intervals from the end of March to the end of October (less regularly at other times). For more information, including timetables and a live 'Ferry-Cam', see www.visitcumbria.com/amb/bowness-ferry.

Tour 19: Typical journey times

By bus (6)
dep Bowness 09.42 to Burnside Hotel
(approx 2 mins)
By foot
from Burnside Hotel to Ferry Nab
(approx 15 mins)
By ferry
dep Ferry Nab 10.10 to Ferry House
(approx 10 mins)
By minibus
dep Ferry House 11.00 to Hawkshead
(approx 15 min)
By minibus
dep Hawkshead 16.20 to Ferry House
(approx 15 mins)
By ferry
dep Ferry House 16.40 to Ferry Nab
(approx 10 mins)
By foot
from Ferry Nab to Burnside Hotel
(approx 15 mins)
By bus (6)
dep Burnside Hotel 17.20 to Bowness
(approx 2 mins)

Note: Bus, rail and ferry timetables can change at very short notice. Be sure to check details before travelling.

During the summer months, a minibus service runs between Ferry House and the village of Hawkshead, calling at Beatrix Potter's Hill Top House. It then runs along the shore of Esthwaite Water, a small lake renowned for its trout fishing as well as for pike and coarse angling. In Hawkshead, connections are available to Grizedale Forest Visitor Centre and Tarn Hows.

The village of **Hawkshead**, situated just to the north of Esthwaite Water, is regarded

WINDERMERE A Furness Railway postcard showing the old ferry at Windermere at the turn of the 20th century.

WINDERMERE
Another view of the ferry circa 1900, with a horse-drawn carriage and passengers. Today, as the Windermere Ferry, it carries cars and passengers from Ferry Nab just south of Bowness to Ferry House at Far Sawrey. The journey across the centre of the lake takes about 10 minutes and runs throughout the year.

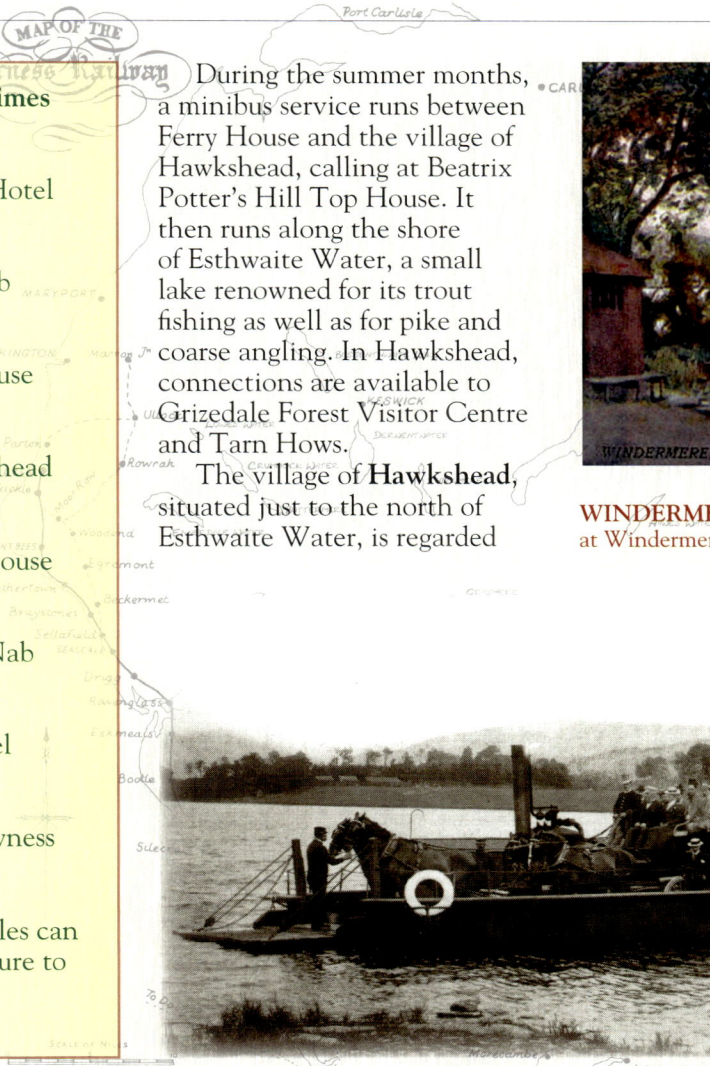

An extract from an 1896 Furness Railway Map

ESTHWAITE WATER Anglers try their luck.

HAWKSHEAD Flag Street is depicted on a Furness Railway postcard, circa 1906. *Ken Norman collection*

as one of the most attractive in the Lake District, with many of its buildings dating back to the 17th century. Its strong connections with Beatrix Potter (being home to the Beatrix Potter Gallery) and William Wordsworth (who attended school here) have made it a magnet for tourists, drawn by its timeless character.

Just south of the village, within walking distance, is **Grizedale Forest**, with its large Visitor Centre. The area is managed by the Forestry Commission and has many attractive way-marked walks, small tarns and some intriguing sculptures scattered throughout.

Also nearby is the local beauty spot

An extract from an 1896 Furness Railway Map

FAR SAWREY The Windermere Ferry arrives at Ferry House, Far Sawrey.

'Near Ferry Nab, Windermere', reproduced from *Beautiful Lakeland* by Ashley P. Abraham (1912).

of **Tarn Hows**, a picturesque tarn with breathtaking views towards the Helvellyn range and the Langdale Pikes. It was designated a Site of Special Scientific Interest in 1965. A well-maintained footpath around the tarn makes for an excellent walk. For further details about this favourite location, see Tour 9, the Tarn Hows Tour (page 128).

The return journey retraces our route, first by minibus from Hawkshead to Ferry House at Far Sawrey, then across the lake

by means of the ferry. If time and the infrequent bus service permit, the luxury of afternoon tea at Storrs Hall is worth considering. Storrs Hall is a smart four-star hotel on the shore of Windermere about 3 miles (5km) south of Bowness. A Grade II listed Georgian mansion in an idyllic setting of 17 acres of gardens, it offers exceptional views of the lake and surrounding mountains. Afternoon tea may be taken in the gardens or the hotel lounges – a treat that was included in the Furness

Railway schedule for this tour, although the cost apparently was not!

Alternatively, the number 6 bus service towards Windermere operated by Stagecoach stops outside the Burnside Hotel (a 15-minute walk from the ferry landing) for the short ride back to Bowness.

An extract from an 1896 Furness Railway Map

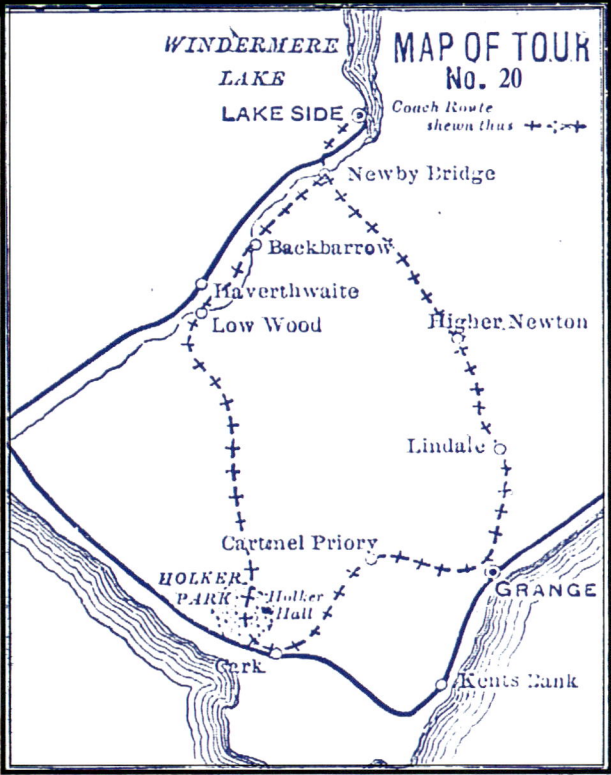

MAP OF TOUR No. 20

WINDERMERE LAKE

LAKE SIDE

Coach Route shewn thus

Newby Bridge

Backbarrow

Haverthwaite

Low Wood

Higher Newton

Lindale

Cartmel Priory

HOLKER PARK

Holker Hall

GRANGE

Cark

Kents Bank

SCALE OF MILES

Tour 20: The Cartmel Priory and Newby Bridge Tour
Grange-Cartmel Priory-Holker Hall-Haverthwaite-Backbarrow-Newby Bridge-Lindale-Grange

By bus or national rail from Grange to Cark for Cartmel Priory (optional) – by foot to Holker Hall and return – by national rail to Ulverston – by bus to Haverthwaite – by heritage railway to Lakeside – by foot to Newby Bridge – by bus to Grange

- Allow about 8 hours for the full itinerary (can be shortened)
- Suggested starting point: Grange-over-Sands, Crown Hill opposite the Post Office

The charming seaside town of **Grange-over-Sands** is a fine location for the start of this interesting circular tour, which involves rail, bus and short walks.

Situated on the Cartmel peninsula, Grange offers fine views across Morecambe Bay while also backed by the attractive peaks of the southern Lakeland fells. Near the railway station are the well-laid-out Ornamental Gardens with mature trees, flowering shrubs, herbaceous borders and lake, which make a tranquil spot to wait for

a bus or train. Until the arrival of the Furness Railway the quickest route from Lancaster was across the sands – a journey fraught with danger! Today, the now popular and bustling town attracts visitors eager to explore this unspoilt area on the edge of the Lake District using safer means of access. For a fuller account of the Grange-over-Sands area, refer to Tour 3, the Grange and Windermere Circular Tour (page 19).

If Cartmel Priory is to be visited, take the bus service 532 from Crown

Tour 20: Typical journey times

By bus (532)
dep Grange 10.33 for Cartmel Priory (approx 10 mins)
By bus (532)
dep Cartmel 12.44 to Cark (approx 5 mins)
By foot
from Cark to Holker Hall (approx 20 mins)
Lunch at Holker Hall
By foot
from Holker Hall 15.50 to Cark (approx 20 mins)
By rail
dep Cark & Cartmel 16.09 to Ulverston (approx 10 mins)
By bus (X6)
dep Ulverston 16.27 to Haverthwaite (approx 10 mins)
By rail (L&HR)
dep Haverthwaite 17.20* to Lakeside (approx 10 mins)
By foot
from Lakeside to Newby Bridge (approx 25 mins) – or quicker by train
By bus (X6)
dep Newby Bridge 18.07 to Grange (approx 20 mins)

*Late afternoon service operates June to August only

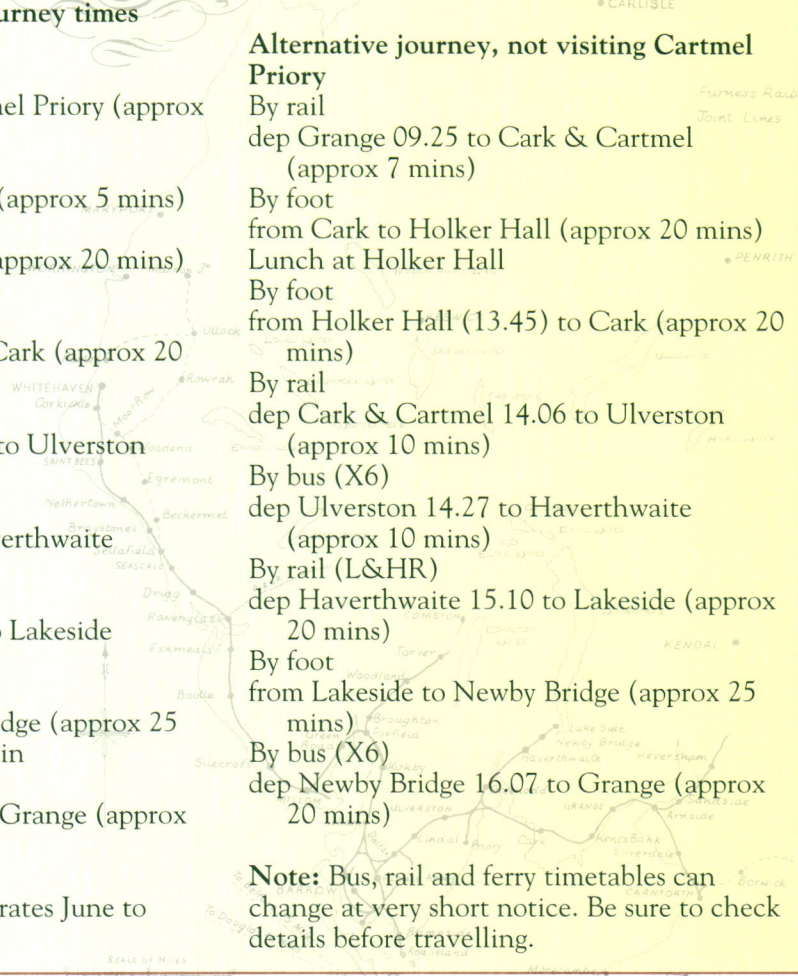

Alternative journey, not visiting Cartmel Priory

By rail
dep Grange 09.25 to Cark & Cartmel (approx 7 mins)
By foot
from Cark to Holker Hall (approx 20 mins)
Lunch at Holker Hall
By foot
from Holker Hall (13.45) to Cark (approx 20 mins)
By rail
dep Cark & Cartmel 14.06 to Ulverston (approx 10 mins)
By bus (X6)
dep Ulverston 14.27 to Haverthwaite (approx 10 mins)
By rail (L&HR)
dep Haverthwaite 15.10 to Lakeside (approx 20 mins)
By foot
from Lakeside to Newby Bridge (approx 25 mins)
By bus (X6)
dep Newby Bridge 16.07 to Grange (approx 20 mins)

Note: Bus, rail and ferry timetables can change at very short notice. Be sure to check details before travelling.

MORECAMBE BAY Looking down from Arnside Knott, with Grange-over-Sands in the distance, a party of walkers is led by an experienced guide, known as a Sand Pilot, across the treacherous sands of Morecambe Bay.

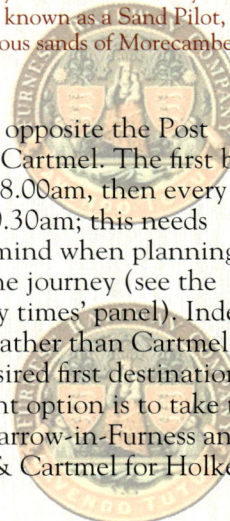

Hill in Grange, opposite the Post Office, towards Cartmel. The first bus leaves at about 8.00am, then every 2 hours from 10.30am; this needs to be borne in mind when planning any breaks in the journey (see the 'Typical journey times' panel). Indeed, if Holker Hall rather than Cartmel Priory is the desired first destination, a more convenient option is to take the train towards Barrow-in-Furness and alight at Cark & Cartmel for Holker

Hall. The train from Grange to Cark hugs the Morecambe Bay coastline, and is a delightful ride in itself.

The bus ride from Grange to **Cartmel Priory** takes about 10 minutes. Founded in 1190 and dissolved in 1536, only the priory church and a gatehouse now survive from the original monastic buildings. The church is still active and is recognised as one of the finest ecclesiastical buildings in the North of England, being designated by English Heritage as a Grade I listed building. **Cartmel** village is 2.3 miles (3.5km) north-west of Grange-over-Sands; originally in Lancashire, it is now in Cumbria. The ancient deanery of Cartmel, together with that of Furness, formed that detached portion of Lancashire known as 'Lancashire North of the Sands', and as mentioned above the main route into the area prior to the coming of the railway

CARK IN CARTMEL An FR postcard of Cark in Cartmel station (as it was then called). To the east of the station there were once carriage sidings where stock from the many 'specials' run to the famous Cartmel Horse Races was stabled throughout the day.

CARK IN CARTMEL At today's Cark & Cartmel station the elaborate lattice footbridge still carries its FR bridge-plate No.27. The station was opened by the Ulverstone & Lancaster Railway Company in 1857 as Cark in Cartmel, and was renamed in 1906 It is still served by the modern-day Furness line, with regular trains to Barrow and Carlisle, as well as to Lancaster, Preston and stations to Manchester Airport.

An extract from an 1896 Furness Railway Map

involved the treacherous 'oversands' crossing of Morecambe Bay by coach or chaise, although virtually all goods and mineral traffic was carried by sea. Cartmel has become known as the 'home of sticky toffee pudding', a delicacy that can be bought in various sizes from the village shop. The popular racecourse here holds meetings two or three times a year.

From the village, a leisurely walk of about 20 minutes brings you to **Holker Hall**, a destination well worth the small effort involved. The walk follows part of the Cistercian Way (Cumbria), a long-distance footpath that runs from Grange-over-Sands to Roa Island, south of Barrow, a distance of 33 miles (53km). Described as 'one of the best-loved stately houses in Britain', Holker Hall is the home of Lord and Lady Cavendish, and formerly that of the Dukes of Devonshire. The Hall and Gardens are open from March to November, and there is a cafe, food-hall and gift shop. Dating from the 16th century with a Grade II listed house, the buildings stand in an estate of about 80 hectares, consisting of formal gardens, parkland and woodland, which is frequently used for activities such as hot-air ballooning, driving trials for horse-drawn carriages and country shows.

CARTMEL The village Church, from a postcard by F. Frith & Co, Reigate, circa 1900.

Cartmel Church.

HOLKER HALL Sunlight scatters from a fountain in the gardens of Holker Hall.

An extract from an 1896 Furness Railway Map

Sadly, the bus route from Holker Hall (Cark) to Newby Bridge at the base of Windermere, by way of Low Wood and Backbarrow, no longer exists, which means we now must walk back to Cark, this time to the railway station, to catch the train to Ulverston operated by Northern Rail, a delightful journey of less than 10 minutes with lovely sea views to enjoy. Once at Ulverston, take the bus to Haverthwaite,

then travel by the Lakeside & Haverthwaite heritage line to Lakeside. For details of the journey from Ulverston to Lakeside see Tour 3, The Grange and Windermere Circular Tour (page 19).

Arriving at the terminus of the Lakeside & Haverthwaite Railway at Lakeside Pier, the excellent and informative Lakes Aquarium can be visited, and there is also a restaurant on the pier offering panoramic

views of Windermere. From here we can stroll through the unspoiled valley of the River Leven to Newby Bridge, an easy walk of about 25 minutes. Alternatively, take the train back to the unstaffed halt of Newby Bridge.

A railway line to Newby Bridge from the junction at Plumpton, to run via Greenodd and Haverthwaite, had been under discussion by the Board of Directors of the Furness Railway since 1847, keen as they were to tap into the lucrative tourist

HAVERTHWAITE Being the headquarters of the heritage line, Haverthwaite boasts an attractive station with restaurant, shop and signal box.

An extract from an 1896 Furness Railway Map

HAVERTHWAITE Across the yard, the company's collection of locomotives and associated stock can be viewed in the shed.

trade founded upon the steamer traffic on Windermere. These passengers were brought in by the Kendal & Windermere Railway, which had reached Birthwaite, later to become the resort of Windermere, in that year. However, it was not until the 1860s that the line materialised, and by then the Directors had decided that a further extension to the deep-water quay at Lake Side would be preferable to using the shallow channel at Newby Bridge. The

new branch, completed in 1869, was double track from Plumpton Junction to Greenodd, then single thereafter, with a passing loop at Haverthwaite. But in those early years passenger receipts were disappointing in spite of the FR's take-over of the Windermere Steam Yacht Company's fleet of steam ships in 1872. It was not until 1896, when Alfred Aslett became General Manager, that the company's tourism policy bore fruit, following his introduction of the

20 new Furness Railway Tours, using charabancs, steamships and, of course, the railway, of which this route is one.

In Newby Bridge the X6 bus service from Kendal departs on an hourly basis from opposite the Swan Hotel. The journey time back to Grange railway station is about 20 minutes.

Right: **LAKESIDE** Very conveniently located beside the station is the Lakes Aquarium.

Below: **NEWBY BRIDGE** is depicted on a Furness Railway postcard.

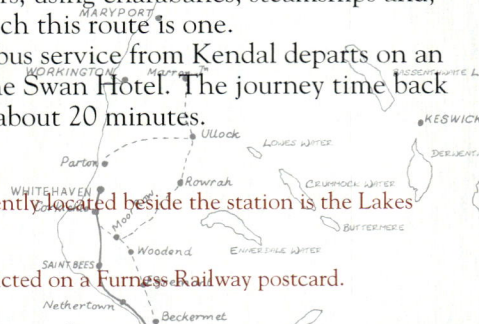

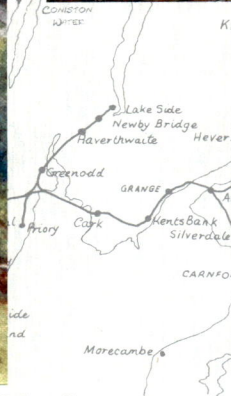

An extract from an 1896 Furness Railway Map

HAVERTHWAITE
An appealing sign at Haverthwaite station in 2003. *John Townsend*

MAP OF CIRCULAR TOUR No. 1

Route by
Rail shewn thus
Boat
Coach

AMBLESIDE
Low Wood
CONISTON
BOWNESS
Tower
Ferry
Storrs Hall
Woodland
LAKE SIDE
Broughton
Haverthwaite
Foxfield Junc.
Greenodd
Kirkby
ULVERSTON
Askam
The Duddon Sands
Lindal
Dalton
FURNESS ABBEY
BARROW
Roose
CONISTON LAKE
WINDERMERE LAKE
MORECAMBE BAY

SCALE OF MILES

To Douglas 46 Miles

An extract from an 1896 Furness Railway Map

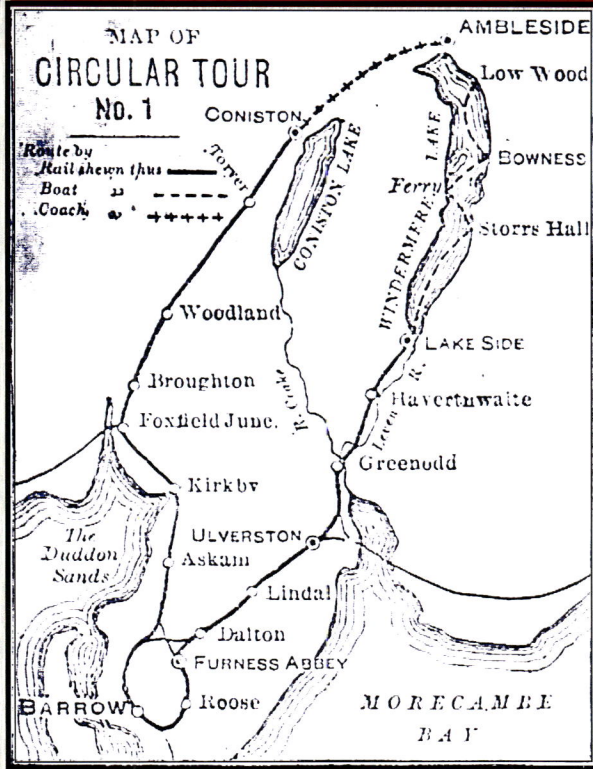

Tour 1: The Outer Circular Tour

Ulverston-Haverthwaite-Windermere-Ambleside-Coniston-Barrow-Furness Abbey-Ulverston

I n Furness Railway days, Tour No 1 was promoted as one to be embarked upon in a 'clockwise' direction, as indicated on the accompanying ticket, with Lakeside, at the southern tip of Windermere, suggested as the starting point for the rail journey by way of Ulverston (see Tour 3 for more details of this section), then from Foxfield Junction along the branch line to Coniston. From here, a coach would carry passengers by way of what is today the A592 and A591 road to Ambleside, where a lake steamer would then be taken to travel the full length of the lake to the starting point at Lakeside. Tour 4 (page 38) has further information on this part of the journey.

The following suggested tour by car illustrates the flexibility

the Circular Tours, being equally enjoyable wherever you join the route. However, our suggested starting point is **Ulverston**. The town is overlooked by a concrete structure built in 1850 known as the Hoad Monument. It commemorates local resident Sir John Barrow, 1st Baronet, Fellow of the Royal Society, Fellow of the Royal Geographical Society, statesman, writer and promoter of Arctic voyages of discovery. The easy walk up to the monument rewards the visitor with splendid scenic views of the surrounding areas, including

WINDERMERE FR postcard: 'Windermere from Wansfell (Sunset)', circa 1906. *Ken Norman collection*

ULVERSTON A postcard view, circa 1910, of the Hoad or Barrow Monument, which stands above Ulverston.

Morecambe Bay and parts of the Lake District.

Start by taking the A590 road from Ulverston to Newby Bridge, by way of Greenodd and Haverthwaite, then turn left to follow the A592 along the eastern shore of Windermere to Bowness. At Bowness, continue along the A592 to pass west of Windermere, then take the A591 to Ambleside. From Ambleside, the A593 runs west then south to **Coniston**, a short distance from the head of the lake.

The 8½-mile (14km) single-track line from Foxfield Junction, through Broughton, Woodland and Torver to Coniston was opened in 1859 by the Coniston Railway Company. Initially used to transport copper ore from the mines above Coniston, this soon proved to be unprofitable and the line became increasingly dependent on tourism. The Coniston Railway was absorbed into the Furness empire in 1862, and the new owners did much to improve the station facilities for visitors, although of course it was the lake that was the major attraction, with steamer services (also operated by the FR) having been introduced two years earlier.

The Coniston branch line (see Tour 4 [page 38] for further information) was pivotal not only to this tour, but also to Tour 2, the Inner Circular Tour, and Tour 7, the Four Lakes Circular Tour, and its closure in 1962 rendered these tours also impossible to follow in their intended manner. In the case of this tour, not only is there no railway to Coniston, but there is also no bus service connecting Coniston directly with Barrow-in-Furness.

Follow the A593 south above Coniston Water, through Torver and on to Broughton in Furness, then turn left to follow the A595 through Grizebeck, where it turns to head south through Askam and Dalton-in-Furness (see below). At Dalton turn right and take the A590 to Barrow.

Prior to 1880, **Barrow-in-Furness** had been at the end of a minor branch line from Dalton passing by Furness Abbey and Roose, with through trains to the north continuing from Dalton along the main line to Askam and on towards Millom, but in that year it was decided to build a loop

through the town, thus putting Barrow on the 'new' main line. In fact, in 1846 Barrow was but a hamlet, even though it was the birthplace of the Furness Railway with its two original routes from Kirkby to Piel on Roa Island, and from Dalton to Barrow focussing on the area.

The most important factor in the remarkable growth of Barrow was undoubtedly the progress of railway development from the 1830s. At first this was slow, but the appointment of James Ramsden from Wolverton Works in 1846 and his later elevation to Superintendent of

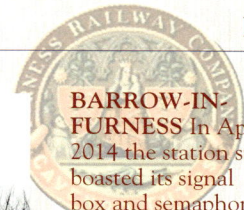

BARROW-IN-FURNESS In April 2014 the station still boasted its signal box and semaphore signals.

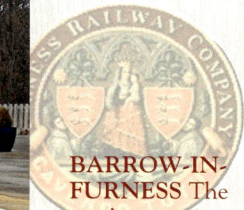

BARROW-IN-FURNESS The area's attractions are illustrated on the platform wall at the recently renovated Barrow station.

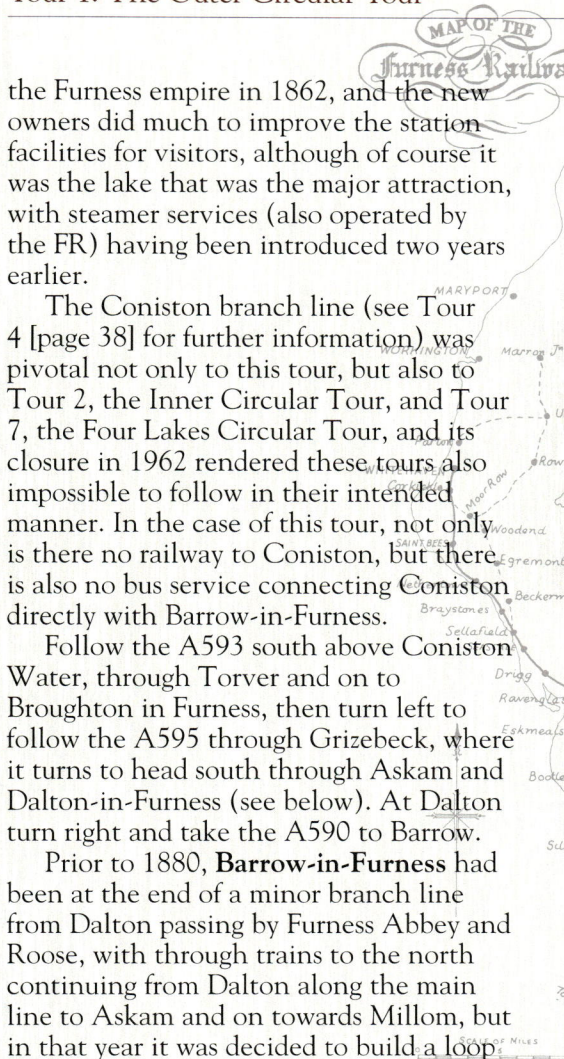

the Line in 1850 resulted in the innovation needed to extend the company's lines, and once the Ulverstone & Lancaster Railway (U&LR) was opened through to Carnforth in 1857 and Henry Schneider opened his first blast furnaces in Barrow in 1859, the scene was set for rapid expansion. During the 1860s the FR absorbed its neighbours one by one, with the U&LR in 1862 and the Whitehaven & Furness Junction Railway in 1866. The company prospered in spite of the economic slumps and depression before the First World War.

From that time, however, the fortunes of Barrow's railway system showed a steady decline as its geographical isolation proved a permanent setback for the port; the industrial centres of Lancashire and Yorkshire were just too far away and the Furness main line was not built for real speed. There was also an insufficient variety of local industry to keep the port busy, and in the end the town relied almost entirely on the shipbuilding industry.

As the local iron ore resources dwindled, so inevitably did the related heavy industries. Askam Ironworks was the first to close in 1919, to be followed by the much larger complex at Barrow in 1963, and finally by the nearby Millom works in 1968. At the docks, once home to steamers operating to the Isle of Man and Belfast, in

BARROW-IN-FURNESS Barrow's Dock Museum occupies the former dry dock, or 'Graving Dock', where three floors contain exhibits and models relating to the history and development of the Barrow area. The term 'graving' refers to the process of waterproofing the hulls of ships by burning off weed and applying coats of tar. The dock was 500 feet (150 metres) long, 60 feet (18 metres) wide and 33 feet (10 metres) deep, and could be emptied of water to allow work to be carried out on vessels of up to 5,500 tons. It was constructed by the FR from sandstone from the nearby Hawcoat Quarries and opened in 1872, continuing in use until the 1950s. Of course, being a product of the enterprise of the Furness Railway Company, the museum also houses several artefacts of local railway interest, including some station furniture, signs and signalling equipment.

An extract from an 1896 Furness Railway Map

BARROW-IN-FURNESS Occupying the lowest floor of the dry dock is the frame of *Nance*, a Morecambe Bay 'prawner' built in 1914 at nearby Arnside. Alongside it is the yacht *White Rose*, a gaff-cutter from the 1880s; built locally in the Ashburner Yard, she competed successfully in district races until the 1980s.

addition to the regular cruises to Fleetwood, it is shipbuilding that has long been the major source of revenue. The Dock Museum in the town describes the history of the area from pre-Viking times to the present day, focussing particularly on the shipbuilding and steel industries, but also including the impact of war on the town and much more of interest. The museum is signposted from the town centre and is open from 11.00am to 4.00pm, Wednesday to Sunday, offering free admission and parking, as well as a cafe and shop. For further information visit www.dockmuseum.org.uk.

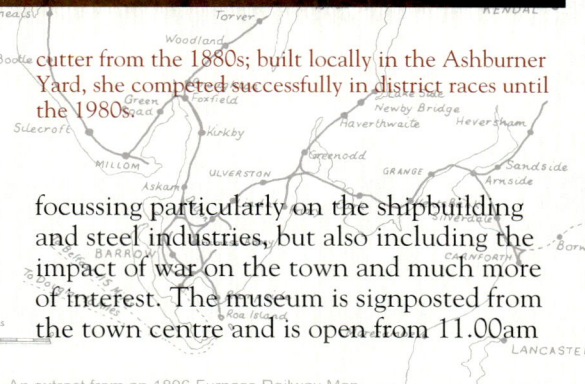

On the northern outskirts of Barrow, located in a peaceful valley known as 'the Valley of the Deadly Nightshade', can be found the majestic remains of the former monastery now known as **Furness Abbey**. Dating back to 1123 in the reign of King Stephen, the abbey was second only to Fountains Abbey in North Yorkshire in terms of its wealth and power within the Cistercian order. The original occupants were a colony of Benedictine monks from Savigney in Normandy, who soon entered the stricter and more austere order of the Cistercians. The abbot ruled supreme in the area for 400 years, until the eventual dissolution of the abbey in 1537, when its stately buildings were reduced while its lands and revenues were annexed to the Duchy of Lancaster. The abbey was located next to the Furness Railway line into Barrow and at one time boasted its own station, but this was closed in 1950, leaving Roose and Dalton as the nearest today. Road access is straightforward, however, as the abbey is conveniently situated at the end of Abbey Road, Barrow's main through road, which links the railway station with the town centre and of course the abbey

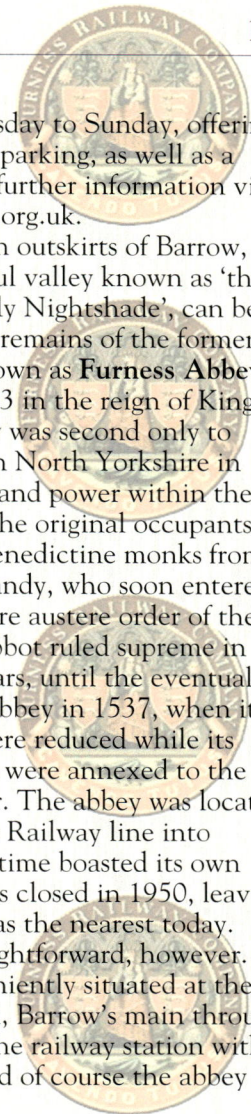

FURNESS ABBEY.

from which it got its name. The site is now in the care of English Heritage, which is involved in the ongoing process of restoration of the impressive sandstone ruins.

A mile (1.6km) from Furness Abbey is the ancient market town of **Dalton-in-Furness**, one time capital of Furness; its castle, dating from the 1330s and used by the abbots to hold their civil courts, is now in the care of the National Trust. Dalton is also the location of the South Lakes Wild Animal Park, which describes itself as 'one of the best conservation zoos in the country' and which has frequently received the 'Top Attraction for Excellence in the Lake District' award since opening in 1994. The park is

Left: **FURNESS ABBEY** A Furness Railway postcard depicting Furness Abbey in 1911.

Below left: **FURNESS ABBEY** The similar viewpoint in April 2003. *J. Townsend*

Below: **FURNESS ABBEY** The impressive ruins of Furness Abbey today.

An extract from an 1896 Furness Railway Map

Furness Station and Abbey Hotel

Left: **FURNESS ABBEY STATION** This FR postcard shows Furness Abbey station and the Abbey Hotel. The station was considered to be the company's most attractive, adjoining the imposing ruins of the Abbey of Saint Mary of Furness. The nearby Furness Abbey Hotel occupied the site of the Manor House and was managed by the company. The domain of the Ramsden family, so closely associated with Barrow and the FR, lay to the east, with a private access winding down through the woodland.

Below right: **FURNESS ABBEY STATION** The station was closed in 1950 and soon demolished. These two views taken in April 2003 show the site of the station looking north towards Dalton and south through the 70-yard Furness Abbey tunnel towards Barrow-in-Furness. *J. Townsend*

Left: **FURNESS ABBEY HOTEL** is seen from the tennis lawn in this Series 17 postcard by Raphael Tuck & Sons Ltd for the Furness Railway, circa 1910. The description on the reverse reads: 'Furness Abbey Hotel, Barrow in Furness. Beautifully situated within the grounds of Furness Abbey and adjoining Furness Abbey Station. Centre for the English Lake District. Within 1½ miles of George Romney's early home.'

An extract from an 1896 Furness Railway Map

Left: **DALTON-IN-FURNESS** Although the station buildings at Dalton-in-Furness have been converted into private homes, the station still functions as a stop on the Furness line between Barrow and Lancaster.

Below right: **DALTON-IN-FURNESS** This cleverly designed modern arch over the platform entrance at Dalton station commemorates the artist George Romney (1734-1802), the most fashionable portrait painter of his day. He was born at Beckside in Dalton and is buried in the churchyard of St Mary's Parish Church in the town. A visit to his home at High Cocken near Barrow, opened to the public as a museum by the FR, could be incorporated into this tour. The arch also carries the dates 1643 and 1846. The former was the date of the Civil War battle at nearby Lindal Close between Cromwell's army and the Royalists, who were defeated and pursued through the town, which was then pillaged and plundered by the victorious army. 1846 was the date the railway arrived in the town.

home to an impressive collection of exotic species of mammals and birds from all continents and is open every day except Christmas Day. For further information visit www.southlakessafarizoo.com.

The nearby National Nature Reserve of Sandscale Haws, with its excellent views over Duddon Sands is open throughout the year, has free entry, a car park, toilets, and extensive well-maintained footpaths.

The A590 takes us back to Ulverston, our starting point. **Ulverston** once boasted a daily 'oversands' coach (at hours varying to suit the tides) across Morecambe Bay

to and from Lancaster, in the days before the building of the Ulverstone & Lancaster Railway, which joined the two by way of Carnforth in 1857. The new railway opened a channel of communication between the hitherto almost isolated lines in the districts of Furness and west Cumberland (as was) and the hives of industry to the south. The short-lived Ulverston & Lancaster Railway was absorbed into the growing Furness Railway empire in 1862.

An extract from an 1896 Furness Railway Map

MAP OF
CIRCULAR TOUR
No. 2

Route by
Rail shewn thus ____
Boat   " ----
Coach   " ++++++

CONISTON
Torver
Woodland
LAKE BANK
Broughton
Foxfield Junc.
Kirkby
GREENODD
ULVERSTON
Askam
Lindal
The Duddon Sands
Dalton
FURNESS ABBEY
BARROW
Roose
Rampside Pier
MORECAMBE BAY

SCALE OF MILES

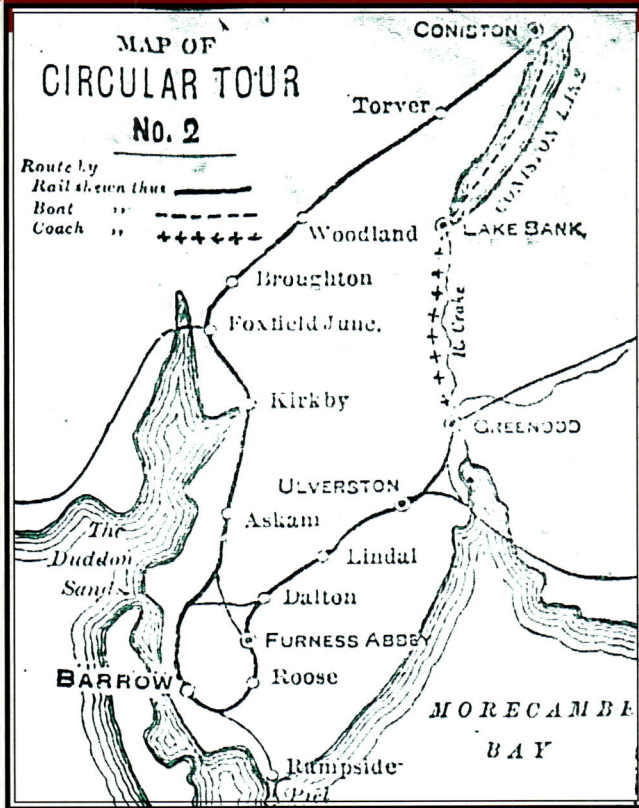

Tour 2: The Inner Circular Tour
Ulverston-Barrow-Coniston-Torver-Greenodd-Ulverston

Tour 2, like Tour 1, could be embarked upon from the railway station at Ulverston, but in this instance one travelled westwards; today's journey by car therefore follows the same route between Ulverston and Coniston as outlined in Tour 1, except in the reverse direction. In Furness Railway days, Tour 1 was often taken in the 'anti-clockwise' direction to allow passengers the experience of the more challenging uphill train journey along the Lake Side branch, whereas Tour 2 took the 'clockwise' route featuring the 'uphill' of the Coniston branch.

Take the A590 road towards Barrow, which follows the railway as it climbs out of Ulverston into the area of Furness that was once covered with iron ore mines, to which the FR owed its origins and later prosperity. **Lindal in Furness** is at the summit of the line, and shortly afterwards is the site of Lindal Ore Sidings, where in 1892 a train crew had to jump for their lives as their locomotive disappeared into a hole in the ground when the tracks fell into mine workings. The FR's Class 'D1' 0-6-0 No 115 was at the head of a Barrow to Carnforth goods train, shunting near the sidings, when

1st and 3rd Class tickets for Tour 2, the Inner Circular Tour, featuring the full complement of FR travel modes.

the driver noticed large cracks opening up beneath the train. The area has a history of mining subsidence and this is usually cited as the explanation for the accident, although an alternative theory is that the loco plunged into a cavity caused by the collapse of an underlying wash hole or sink hole, of which the Furness area has many. Whatever the reason, the loco

BARROW-IN-FURNESS A terminating service from Manchester Oxford Road, 1C51, arrives at Barrow-in-Furness station on 3 April 2014, formed by First TransPennine Express Class 185 'Desiro' three-car DMU No 185146. The station has been

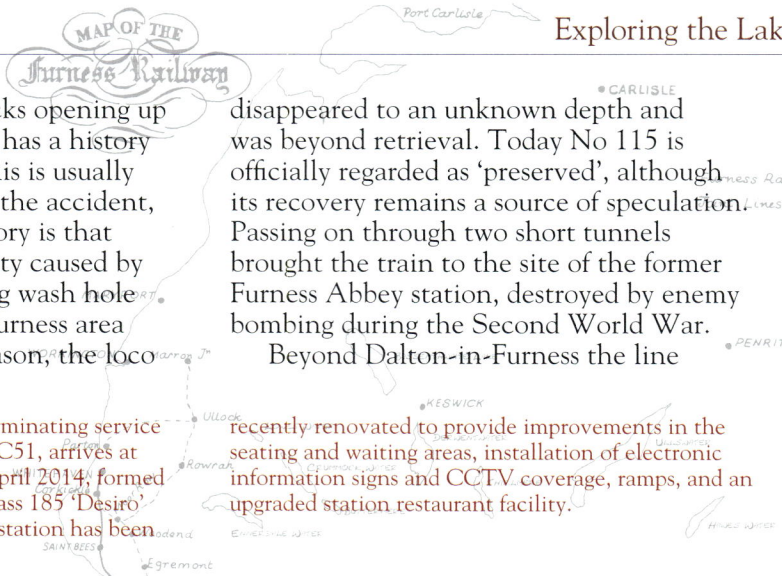

disappeared to an unknown depth and was beyond retrieval. Today No 115 is officially regarded as 'preserved', although its recovery remains a source of speculation. Passing on through two short tunnels brought the train to the site of the former Furness Abbey station, destroyed by enemy bombing during the Second World War.

Beyond Dalton-in-Furness the line

recently renovated to provide improvements in the seating and waiting areas, installation of electronic information signs and CCTV coverage, ramps, and an upgraded station restaurant facility.

completes an almost full circle, the 'Dalton Loop', in order to include the town of **Barrow-in-Furness**, whose station had to be rebuilt by BR following enemy action in the same conflict. Barrow is described in more detail in Tour 1 (page 99).

By the 1960s a variety of steam locos could still be observed at work in the Barrow area, including Stanier 'Black 5s' from Carnforth, Lostock Hall or Wigan Springs Branch depots, Fowler 4F 'Compounds' from Workington, Ivatt Class 2 and Class 4 'Moguls', also from Carnforth or Wigan Springs Branch, and the numerous Class 4 2-6-4 tanks designed by Fowler, Stanier or Fairburn and operating out of Barrow, Carnforth or Lancaster Green Ayre sheds. In the summer months these 'locals' might be augmented by visitors from further afield, perhaps one of the surviving 'Jubilees' from the Leeds area with an excursion to Windermere. However, by this time the effects of the 1955 BR Modernisation Plan were being felt throughout the country, and even in the more remote North West the diesels were beginning to have an impact. The Barrow area received the full complement of 20 Metropolitan-Vickers Type 2 (BR Class 28) Co-Bo locos built in the late 1950s, with their wheel arrangement unique among British designs. Transferred from the Midland Division, they became a familiar sight on the coastal line, but with limited route availability and engines prone to breaking down they had been withdrawn by the end of 1969 after only 11 years in

service. One has survived into preservation, No D5705 having been granted a second lease of life to work on the East Lancashire Railway heritage line.

Little now remains of the once extensive network of lines in the Barrow area, and indeed the town itself can be bypassed by trains following the avoiding line from Dalton to rejoin the main line at Park South Junction, from where the line runs north through Askam and Kirkby-in-Furness to Foxfield station, junction for the former branch to Coniston.

After visiting Barrow if desired, we too follow the railway north through Askam by means of the A595 road, pausing at **Foxfield**. The station here is now a 'request stop', and the single island platform boasts an impressive half-timbered signal box. From here visitors in FR days would have taken the Coniston branch through Broughton, Woodland and Torver. The line opened between Broughton and Coniston in 1859, to serve the copper mines at Coniston, though these deposits soon became worked out, leaving the railway dependent on slate, general goods and

Above: Perhaps in competition for the same business in the 1960s, Stanier 4P 2-6-4T No 42656 was built at Derby Works in February 1941 and worked throughout the North West until being withdrawn in May 1967 and cut up at Cashmore's yard, Great Bridge, later that year.

Right: The sole survivor of the 20 'Metro-Vick' Type 2s, whose classmates were scrapped after less than half that time in service, No D5705 is resplendent in preservation during 2011. *Phil Sangwell*

Above: **ASKHAM** The A595 road crosses the railway at Askham by a level crossing, seen here in quieter times in a Furness Railway postcard.

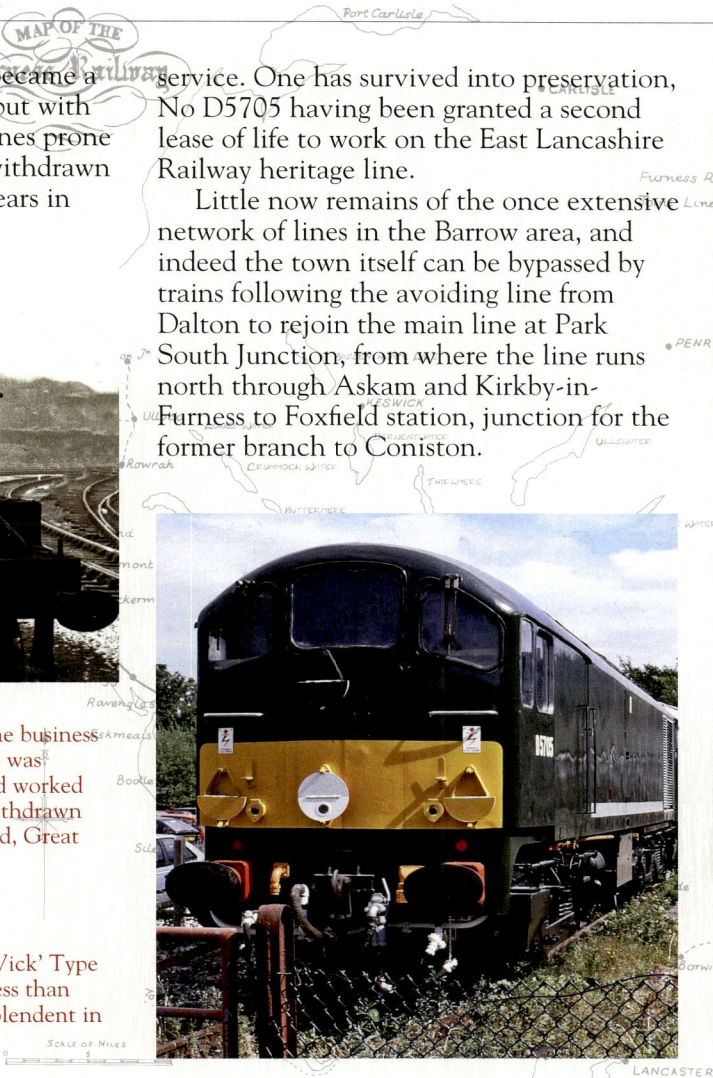

An extract from an 1896 Furness Railway Map

the tourist traffic in the summer season. (For more on the Coniston branch see Tour 4, page 38.)

The area around the village of Coniston had been known for its copper deposits since before the Romans occupied the region more than 2,000 years ago, and archaeological research suggests that the workings might date back to the Bronze Age. In the 18th and 19th centuries the Coniston copper mines were the largest in the North of England. Since then, Coniston Green Slate has been and still is an important local resource, being mined now mainly from Brossen Stone Quarry on the face of the 'Old Man'.

Coniston Water, 5½ miles (9km) long, half a mile (800m) wide and having a maximum depth of 186 feet (56 metres), became greatly polluted by material from the copper mines, all but wiping out the once thriving stocks of char and trout. Happily, the populations of these fish are recovering and a limited number of fishing licences are now being issued.

Though the Coniston Railway began at Broughton, its junction with the Furness Railway proper was at Foxfield station, opened on 1 August 1850 on the edge of the Duddon Estuary. Broughton station had been opened for passenger traffic in 1848, and from 1850 was operated jointly by the

Whitehaven & Furness Junction and the Furness Railway companies.

As with Tour 1, the present-day lack of public transport on this route prevents the tour from being followed as originally intended, so we follow the route of the branch line using the A593 from Broughton in Furness.

The Coniston branch rose steeply at a maximum grade of 1 in 49 to a level crossing provided over the Ulverston road. Thereafter it continued to rise, though

less steeply (a maximum of 1 in 81) to Woodland station, a distance of about 3 miles (5km) from Broughton. Here the station, perched on the side of a hill overlooking the wild and rocky landscape of Subberthwaite, provided a passing place with a waiting shelter and signal box dating from 1896.

The summit of the branch was reached about half a mile (800m) short of **Torver**, about 6 miles (10km) from Broughton. Here the small station with passing loop

FOXFIELD signal box at the station beside the Duddon Estuary.

An extract from an 1896 Furness Railway Map

and goods yard was a collecting point for slate, with storage sidings for the occasional rake of FR ultramarine carriages. The single platform had convenient and direct access through a wicket gate to the local hostelry, The Church House Inn, popular with travellers.

After Torver, the branch rolled mainly downhill to the terminus at Coniston station, sited inconveniently for passengers above the village, though giving easy access to the copper mine wharf and offering superb views over the village and lake, now at about 8 miles from Broughton. As at many other stations where Furness Railway passengers stopped during their tours, the company provided refreshment facilities, offering lunch or tea supplied by the regular FR caterers, Spiers & Pond of London.

Timetables for the early years (for example, May 1865) show five trains per day leaving Barrow and travelling by way of Furness Abbey to Foxfield Junction, to arrive at Coniston 1 hour 10 minutes later, although those services that offered 'request stops' en route took considerably longer, extending the journey time to more than 2 hours. Most trains consisted of 'mixed' passenger and freight vehicles. By LMS days, the weekday service over the branch had been expanded to ten trains each way, including a summer service from Blackpool and, on Saturdays, from Morecambe. A more limited service of six trains was provided on summer Sundays, catering for those seeking to visit the fells and lakes. In addition, one train, the 'Coniston Goods' from Carnforth (later a Barrow working), ran daily, although this was later reduced to Mondays, Wednesdays and Fridays only,

TORVER The Church House Inn at Torver is still a popular stopping off point, while the nearby Wilson's Arms, seen here, also offers a warm welcome to the traveller. Both have an appetising menu and a choice of beverages. They include beers from highly regarded micro-breweries.

The Wilson's Arms, on our visit, featured ales from the Coniston Brewing Company, established in 1995 and located at the popular 400-year-old coaching inn, the Black Bull Inn and Hotel in nearby Coniston. Among award-winning beers is the company's 'Bluebird Bitter', awarded 'Supreme Champion Beer of Britain' in 1998 and the recipient of further accolades in recent years. The company's 'Old Man Ale' is another firm favourite with customers.

An extract from an 1896 Furness Railway Map

Below: Nr TORVER Parts of the Coniston branch trackbed near Torver, though overgrown, are still negotiable and the sturdy road bridges built by the Furness Railway still stand.

Right: Nr TORVER Criss-crossing what remains of the Coniston branch near Torver, minor roads provide stunning views of the surrounding fells and it is not uncommon to come across local produce offered for sale from wayside stalls, their owners relying on the honesty of the traveller to leave money for their purchases.

Below: This is one such farm stall with a tempting selection of jams, chutneys, eggs and butter, together with 'cakes at the weekend'.

until the line was closed to all traffic in April 1962. The track was lifted the following year.

From Torver we follow the A593 on to **Coniston**. Just north of Coniston Water and carrying the A593 road on towards Ambleside is the beautiful valley of Yewdale, with Holme Fell at its head. 'Its glorious jungle of juniper and birch, heather and bracken, make this one of the most attractive of Lakeland's Fells,' wrote Wainwright. Running into the valley from the Tilberthwaite Fells is Yewdale Beck, which flows into Coniston Water. The narrow gorge of Tilberthwaite Gill down a signposted lane from the main road was much visited in the Victorian era, when it was equipped with ladders and

CONISTON WATER The elegant steam yacht *Gondola* can be admired as she sails down the lake from Coniston towards Torver. She has been described as 'the perfect combination of a Venetian gondola and the English steam yacht.'

balconies for the visitors. To the west of Coniston village rise the Coniston Fells, dominated by the 'benevolent giant' of the Old Man (see Tour 4, the Middle Circular Tour, for more details).

From Coniston village, a cruise aboard the steam yacht *Gondola* would transport passengers down the lake to its southern end at Lake Bank, there to transfer to a coach for the journey by road to Greenodd. A short rail journey would then deliver them back to their starting point at Ulverston railway station. So successful was *Gondola* that a second steamer, *Lady of the Lake*, was added in 1907. For more details about Coniston and the journey from there to Ulverston by boat and bus, see Tour 4, the Middle Circular Tour (page 38).

We return along the A593 above the western shore of the lake as far as Torver, where we turn left to follow the A5084 south. This road skirts the southern end of the lake through High and Low Water End, then meets the A5092 at Lowick Green for the short stretch to Greenodd. Turn right at Greenodd on to the A590, which takes us back to Ulverston.

For those seeking an even more pleasant and attractive journey south from Coniston, follow the B5285 towards

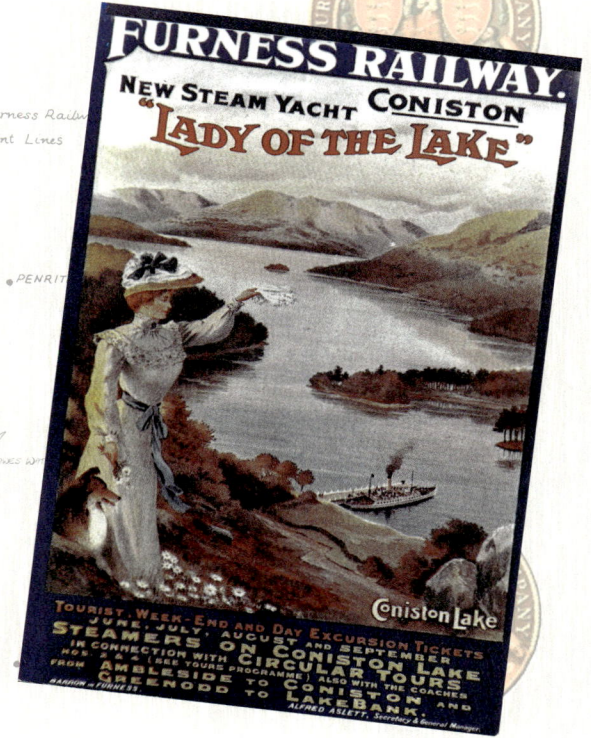

Hawkshead around the northern shore of the lake, then turn south along a minor road that hugs the quieter eastern shore for its entire length, running almost parallel with the A5084 at its southern and, before joining it at Lowick Bridge. A lovely drive.

YEWDALE An FR postcard view of 1913.

Far right: Lady of the Lake depicted on an FR poster.

MAP OF THE
Furness Railway

MAP OF
GRASMERE **CIRCULAR TOUR**
No. 5

GRASMERE LAKE

Route by Coach
shewn thus ++ +++
Steamer

Red Bank

RYDAL WATER

RYDAL

ELTER WATER

LOUGHRIGG TARN

Skelwith Force

R. Brathay

R. Rothay

AMBLESIDE

Clappersgate

Waterhead

WINDERMERE LAKE

Low Wood

SCALE OF MILES

An extract from an 189...

Grasmere Tour
Ambleside-Waterhead-Elter Water-Red Bank-Grasmere-Rydal-Ambleside

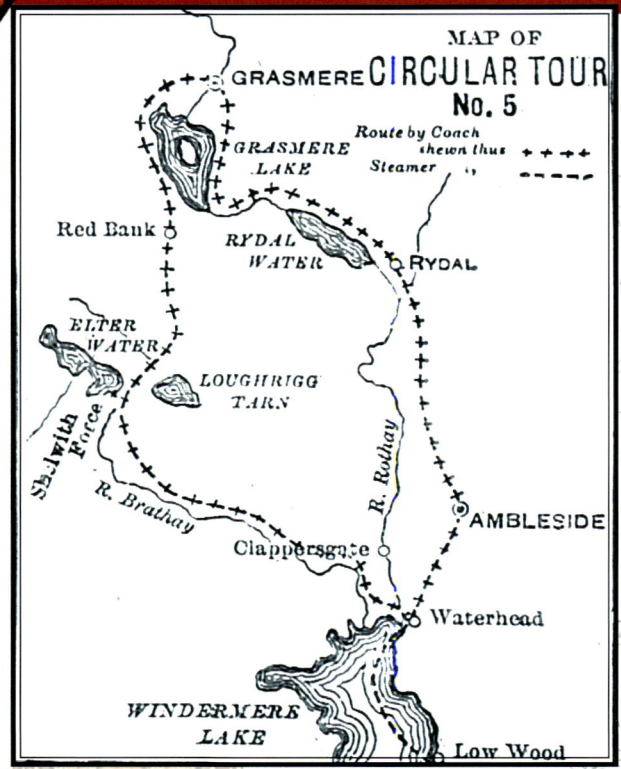

This is one of several tours offered by the Furness Railway that did not have a 'rail element' included, although in common with most of the others it did offer a lake cruise aboard one of its steamers. Waterhead, at the northern extremity of Windermere, was a suggested starting place, though this is now referred to as 'Ambleside Pier'. From here, a return steamer cruise was suggested to Low Wood, now the site of a hotel and water sports centre, though this could be extended as desired, perhaps down to Bowness to make a return cruise of about 1 hour. On returning to Waterhead, a coach would be taken to Grasmere by way of Elter Water and Red Bank, returning via Rydal and Ambleside. Today, cruises are operated by Windermere Lake Cruises and depart from Ambleside Pier (Waterhead) at regular intervals throughout the year, calling at the Lake District Visitor Centre at Brockhole, then Bowness and on to Lakeside at the southern end of the lake. The full journey time from Ambleside to Lakeside is about an hour.

AMBLESIDE PIER
or 'Waterhead', lies at the northern end of Windermere.

Left top to bottom: These Furness Railway postcards show the steam yachts *Cygnet* and *Teal* off Ambleside, SY *Tern* in Bowness Bay in 1912, and SY *Tern* leaving Lake Side Pier.

Below: **SKELWITH BRIDGE**, from a postcard by S. Hildesheimer & Co Ltd, circa 1900.

From Ambleside, our route takes us west along the A593, following the River Brathay, whose waters rise in the wild heights of Wrynose Pass before flowing through Blea Tarn, over the substantial Colwith Force in Little Langdale, then entering **Elter Water** on its way eventually to Windermere. At a point beyond Clappersgate, at Skelwith Bridge, the B5343 branches off to the right towards Elter Water and Langdale, leading to

Skelwith Bridge

An extract from an 1896 Furness Railway Map

SKELWITH FORCE, Langdale, from a postcard by Raphael Tuck & Sons Ltd for the Furness Railway, Series 3, circa 1900.

Skelwith Force, about half a mile (800m) south-east of Elter Water. This stretch of the River Brathay is popular with canoeists, and the 5-metre falls and nearby larger falls of Colwith Force (12 metres) make great locations for practising your camera skills. You can also take in the picturesque Little Langdale Tarn, which although having no direct public access can be viewed easily from the road.

After visiting Elter Water, turn right off the B5343 towards the tiny village of Oaks and **Loughrigg Tarn**, described by Wordsworth as 'a most beautiful example', while Wainwright described the nearby Loughrigg Fell, noting that it had 'no pretensions to mountain form', though he praised its grassy paths as having charming vistas, little tarns and stately trees, adding that 'no ascent is more repaying for the small labour involved'.

The minor road heading north over **Red Bank** towards Grasmere is no longer accessible as a bus route. We follow it along the western shore of Grasmere with the bulk of Silver Fell to our left, with its rough slopes and waterfalls described by Wainwright as 'a lovely name for a lovely fell', saying that he thought it 'landscape artistry at its best'. The road now takes us around the northern shore of **Grasmere** to the village of the same name, a most popular tourist destination associated with the Lake Poets and William Wordsworth in particular, who described it as 'the loveliest spot that man hath ever found'. Overlooking the village to the north-west is the low fell of Helm Crag, whose distinctive summit is easily recognised as the 'Lion and the Lamb'.

Head south from Grasmere village along the A591, skirting the lake again before coming

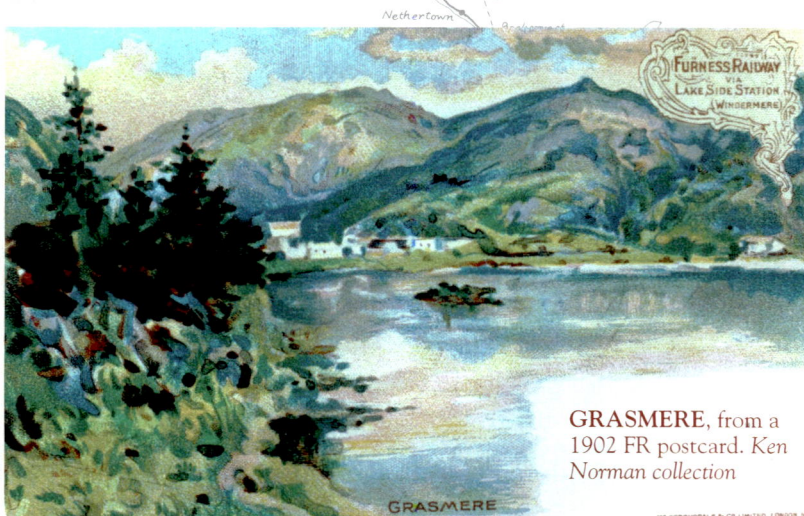

GRASMERE, from a 1902 FR postcard. *Ken Norman collection*

An extract from an 1896 Furness Railway Map

Left: **RYDAL WATER** The tranquil setting of Rydal Water, with the well-known formation of the 'Lion and the Lamb' reflected on its surface.

Below: **GRASMERE** William Wordsworth's Dove Cottage at Grasmere, now a museum, from an FR postcard, circa 1906. *Ken Norman collection*

upon its smaller neighbour, Rydal Water. This is popular walking country. A stroll around the lake takes in both Dove Cottage and Wordsworth's Seat. See Tour 12, the Derwentwater (Keswick) Tour (page 45), for further details. From Rydal, our route takes

us down the attractive valley of the River Rothay, back to Ambleside.

GRASMERE 'A Room in Dove Cottage', reproduced from *Some Portraits of the Lake Poets and their Homes* by G. P. Abrahams, published in Keswick in 1920.

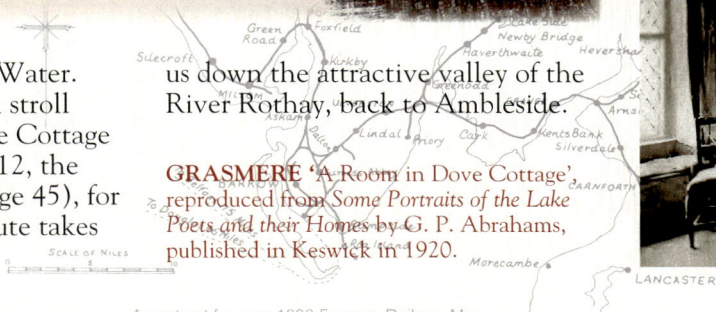

MAP OF
**CIRCULAR TOUR
No. 6**

Thirlspot

THIRLMERE

Route by Coach shewn thus ++++
Steamer ,, ------

Helvellyn 2113

Wythburn

GRASMERE

GRASMERE RYDAL WATER RYDAL

Red Bank AMBLESIDE

ELTERWATER Waterhead

R. Brathay

WINDERMERE

SCALE OF MILES

An extract from an 1896 Furness Railway Map

Tour 6: The Thirlmere, Grasmere and Windermere Tour
Ambleside-Waterhead-Grasmere-Thirlmere-Grasmere-Rydal-Ambleside

Like the previous tour, Tour 6 featured no rail element but in the same way suggested a lake cruise by Furness Railway steamer on Windermere (see Tour 5 above for details). The beginning and the end sections of this tour follow the same routes as Tour 5, but from Grasmere the Furness Railway coach continued northwards to Wythburn and around Thirlmere, which today has no access by public transport.

Follow the route of Tour 5 from Ambleside to Grasmere village via Skelwith Bridge and Red Bank, but now drive north from the village along the A591 towards Thirlmere, following the River Rothay up the pass towards its highest point of Dunmail Raise. To the west rises the massif of High Raise, while to the east the lofty outline of Seat Sandall soars gracefully, dominating the local landscape. Immediately south of **Thirlmere**, at the tiny village of Steel End, turn left onto a minor road that runs northwards alongside the reservoir. With Thirlmere

GRASMERE 'Grasmere Church', an FR postcard, circa 1906. *Ken Norman collection*

GRASMERE CHURCH.   AMBLESIDE STATION.

on our right, the high ground of Brown Rigg, Armboth Fell and finally High Seat dominate the skyline to the west.

After about 2 miles (3.2km), a footpath/bridleway will be seen on the left, which leads across the fell to **Watendlath Tarn**. The small and secluded hamlet of Watendlath and its surroundings were once owned by Furness Abbey, and have been described as 'an exceedingly remote little valley lying among the higher hills above Borrowdale'. A popular starting point from which to explore the surrounding fells, the hamlet consists of a scattering of old farmhouses, now owned by the National Trust, which also operates a tea room, and a highly picturesque stone packhorse bridge over Watendlath beck.

Driving on, when you reach the northern end of Thirlmere, the minor road rejoins the A591. Turn right and head south towards Ambleside along the eastern shore. The skyline to our left is soon dominated by that most climbed of all Lakeland peaks, Helvellyn.

At the southern end of Thirlmere we come to what remains of the village of **Wythburn** – a picturesque church and a small group of houses – the rest of the village having been submerged by the construction of the reservoir at the end of the 19th century. The Thirlmere Aqueduct,

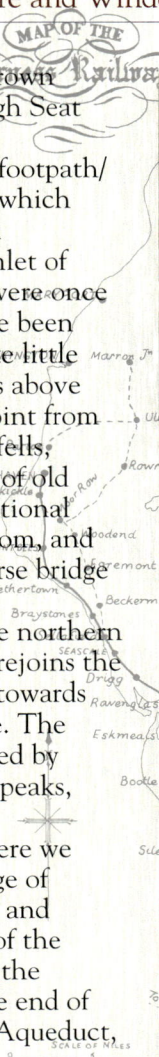

WATENDLATH TARN The peaceful and remote setting of the tarn is approached from a footpath over the fells from Thirlmere. The tarn, see here in October 1987, is well stocked with brown and rainbow trout, making it a favourite fly-fishing water.

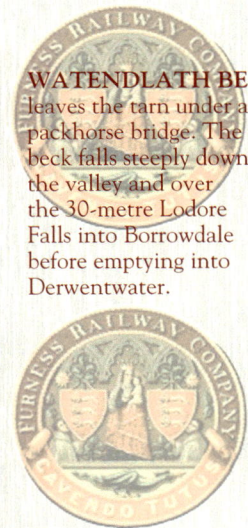

WATENDLATH BECK leaves the tarn under a packhorse bridge. The beck falls steeply down the valley and over the 30-metre Lodore Falls into Borrowdale before emptying into Derwentwater.

about 100 miles (160km) in length, carries the water to Manchester, passing under the pass at Dunmail Raise. The little church contains interesting stained glass windows and an exhibition on the history of the area. Wythburn is also the start of a popular ascent of Helvellyn. Refer to Tour 12, the Derwentwater (Keswick) Tour (page 45), for further information.

Continuing south, we now retrace our journey back to Grasmere, then on through Rydal to Ambleside (see Tour 5 for details of this last section).

THIRLMERE 'Thirlmere & Helvellyn' – an FR postcard from circa 1906. *Ken Norman collection*

THIRLSPOT The Kings Head Hotel at Thirlspot, on the A591 on the eastern shore of Thirlmere, is a former 17th-century coaching inn. Five miles (8km) south of Keswick, Thirlspot sits at the foot of Helvellyn.

An extract from an 1896 Furness Railway Map

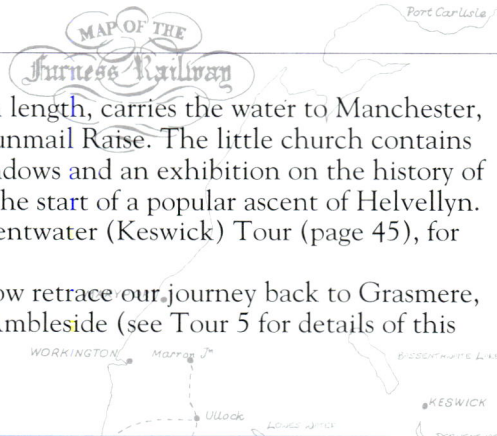

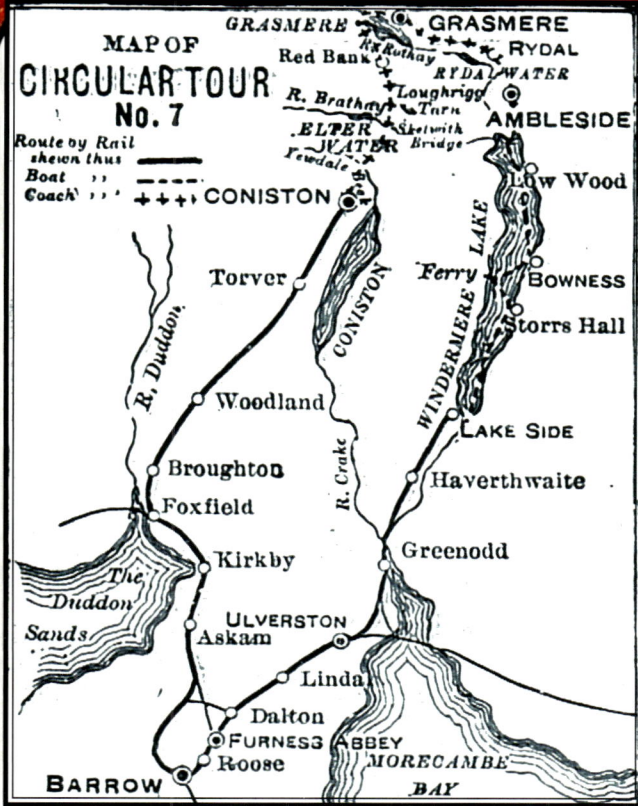

MAP OF
CIRCULAR TOUR
No. 7

Route by Rail
shewn thus
Boat ,,
Coach ,,

Tour 7: The Four Lakes Circular Tour

Ulverston-Greenodd-Haverthwaite-Bowness-Ambleside-Rydal-
Grasmere-Coniston-Foxfield-Barrow-Ulverston

This circular tour encompasses several of the favourite locations and journeys incorporated into the Furness Railway's schedule and much of the route is covered in detail in the itinerary of earlier tours, to which the reader will be referred.

In FR days, the passengers would have begun the tour at Ulverston railway station, from where they would have travelled by train up the Lake Side branch to the foot of Windermere, there to transfer to the waiting steamer for a cruise up the lake to Ambleside. At Ambleside, they would have transferred to a coach for the ride to Grasmere by way of Rydal. Lunch would probably have been taken in Grasmere before boarding the coach again for the journey south via Elter Water to Coniston. At Coniston

RYDAL WATER A Furness Railway postcard.

village, the train would have taken them back down the branch line to Foxfield Junction where they would have joined the company's main line for the journey back to Ulverston by way of Barrow-in-Furness.

Today there is no public transport between Ambleside and Coniston following the route taken by the tour, and the Coniston branch railway is also no more. The journey from Ulverston to Ambleside by car is described in Tour 1, the Outer Circular Tour (page 99), and from Ambleside to Elter Water in Tour 5, the Red Bank and Grasmere Tour (page 114). After passing Elter Water, continue eastwards along the B5343 to its junction with the A593 Ambleside to Coniston road at Skelwith Bridge, a distance of only about a mile (1.6km), then turn right onto this main road and follow it back to Coniston village.

A couple of miles south of Skelwith Bridge, a diversion could be made along the minor road on the right leading over Wrynose Pass into the Duddon Valley. This is the old Welna Scar road, which joins Skelwith Bridge with Broughton in Furness. Between Wrynose and Broughton is the village of **Seathwaite** (not to be confused with the village of the same name just south of Keswick). A colourful local parson known as 'Wonderful Walker' held

SEATHWAITE CHAPEL, reproduced from *The Old Man, or Ravings and Ramblings round Conistone*, published in Kendal by J. Hudson in 1849.

sway here between 1736 and 1802, and when not preaching or teaching classes he worked on local farms, spun wool, and brewed and sold beer until he died at the ripe old age of 92. The local church was restored in Victorian times, and the 16th-century Newfield Inn is a welcome refreshment stop.

Coniston itself consisted of two parts.

'Church Conistone', a chapelry in the parish of Ulverston, lay west of the lake and Yewdale Beck, and extended to Torver in one direction and to Fellfoot in the other. The other part, around the uppermost reaches of the lake, for half a mile down its western shore and 2-3 miles down its eastern shore, was called 'Monk Conistone', and formed part of the parish of

Hawkshead. This whole area of the Furness region was historically part of the county of Lancashire, though divided from the rest by the expanse of Morecambe Bay, thus being known as 'Lancashire beyond the Sands' or 'Lancashire over the Sands' (as in Grange-over-Sands), until in 1974 Furness became part of the new shire county of Cumbria.

The journey from Coniston back to Ulverston via Barrow is detailed in Tour 1 (page 99). About a mile (1.6km) south of Coniston, near the village of Bowmanstead, look out for signs on the left to **Coniston Hall** marina and camping site. The Hall is an imposing 16th-century house on the lake shore, built by the Le Fleming family who made their fortune from copper-mining. Their nearby quay was used to load the ore into barges to be sailed down the lake and from there taken by road to the port of Greenodd to be shipped on for smelting. Today the Hall is owned by the National Trust and is a Grade II listed building, but is not open to the public, although good views can be had from the public footpath. The surrounding area is used as a camping site and the Hall itself houses a variety of

CONISTON Entering Coniston by Yewdale bridge, an engraving from the same source.

CONISTONE HALL.

CONISTON HALL with the 'Old Man' in the background – another 1849 engraving.

An extract from an 1896 Furness Railway Map

tourism enterprises including the booking office for the marina. A walk along the well-maintained footpath to explore the woods of nearby Park Coppice is worthwhile, though unfortunately the most attractive waterside land is not accessible.

Opposite, across Coniston Water, is **Brantwood**, a country house open to the public, administered by a charitable trust and designated a Grade II listed building by English Heritage. It is now a museum dedicated to the hugely influential writer, arts patron, social thinker and philanthropist John Ruskin (1819-1900), who bought the property in 1871 and used the estate as a site for his practical schemes and experiments. He died here of influenza and is buried in Coniston churchyard.

CONISTON HALL today. This imposing house is situated beside the lake on the Cumbria Way.

BRANTWOOD, one-time home of John Ruskin, is seen across Coniston Water in this FR postcard of circa 1906.

CONISTON LAKE & BRANTWOOD (Char Fishing).   **CONISTON STATION.**

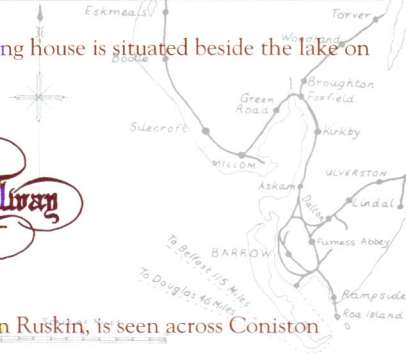

An extract from an 1896 Furness Railway Map

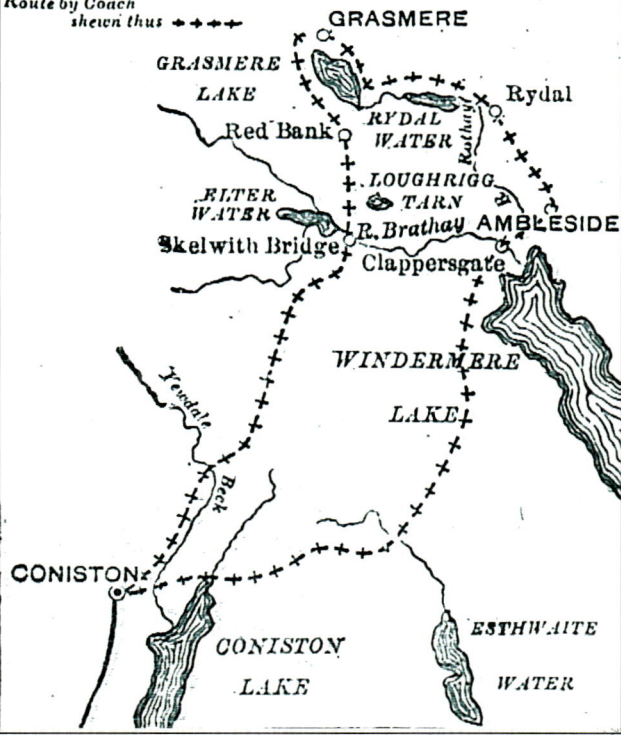

MAP OF TOUR
No. 8

Route by Coach
shewn thus ╈╈╈╈

An extract from an 1896 Furness Railway Map

Tour 8: The Coniston to Coniston Tour
Ambleside-Coniston-Skelwith Bridge-Red Bank-Grasmere-Rydal-Ambleside

The Coniston area is beautiful, with the lake itself, about 6 miles (10km) in length, having its northern end enclosed by magnificent mountains. Hawkshead is 2 miles (3.2km) away, with its own pretty lake, Esthwaite Water, while Ambleside is 5 miles (8km) distant, and a focal point in Furness Railway days for tourists coming by coach from all directions.

This tour and Tour 9 that follows are unusual in that they made use only of the Furness Railway Company's coach operations, having no rail or lake steamer section at all. Instead, they sought to provide the traveller with an opportunity to experience the more remote valleys and fells, where the iron road had never penetrated. It will come as no surprise that today some of these routes are not covered by public bus services, but the journey by car is easy and rewarding. The route of the original tour as operated by the FR started and finished at Coniston, and being a circular tour this option can of course still be followed. The variation proposed here begins and ends at the popular tourist destination of Ambleside and is extended to feature Blelham Tarn and Wray Castle.

From Ambleside, follow the A593 west towards Coniston, but after about a mile (1.6km) turn left at Clappersgate onto the B5286 towards Hawkshead. This will take us near the reed-fringed fishery of **Blelham Tarn**, owned by the National Trust. The waters hold good stocks of perch and roach, but it is for pike that most anglers visit the tarn. Fishing is limited to members of the Windermere, Ambleside & District Angling Association, but to visit the tarn follow the B5286 for about 2 miles (3.2km) then turn left, signposted High Wray and follow this minor road to the entrance to Wray Castle, just south of which a public footpath leads to the tarn. Built in 1840, Wray Castle is a National Trust property open to the public between April and early November, the grounds being open throughout the year.

If not visiting Blelham Tarn or Wray Castle, continue along the B5286 to its junction with the B5285 north of Hawkshead, and turn right towards Coniston village. At Coniston, turn north along the A593, as if returning to Ambleside. We follow the valley of Yewdale Beck, with Yewdale Fells rising abruptly on our left. After about 5 miles (8km) we come to **Skelwith Bridge**, where we turn left to follow the B5343 towards Elter Water, with Skelwith Force to our left. This part of our route to Grasmere via Red Bank and back to Ambleside by way of Rydal is described in Tour 5, the Red Bank and Grasmere Tour (page 114).

As this tour is one of the shorter ones, it allows time for exploration of the area on foot, if desired. Coniston village is a favoured starting point for a number of short walks, up to 5 miles (8km) or so, including one that can be started from the old station car park. It follows the grassy former railway trackbed to Haws Bank, then turns uphill beside the church to go under the old railway line and from there onwards and upwards to Levens Water, where evidence of the former mining industry can still be seen.

Above: **BLELHAM TARN**, beside which is the small National Nature Reserve of Blelham Bog, important for its post-glacial peat deposits as well as its unusual flora, including aromatic bog myrtle, marsh violet and white-beaked sedge.

Left: **WRAY CASTLE,** a National Trust mock-Gothic property, stands on the shore of Windermere, and free guided tours give the visitor its full story.

An extract from an 1896 Furness Railway Map

SKELWITH FORCE COTTAGE.

AMBLESIDE OR CONISTON STATIONS.

Left: **SKELWITH FORCE**, from an FR postcard, circa 1906. One of the smaller Lake District waterfalls, it is also one of the easiest to reach, yet it remains relatively unknown and little visited.

Below: **CONISTON** The walk south from the old station car park quickly leaves the village, but a glance back reminds us how much Coniston is dominated by the 'Old Man'.

Right and below right: **CONISTON** Passing through a short tunnel we are soon rewarded with fine views over the lake.

Further south along the A593 at the village of Torver, the A5084 branches left towards Ulverston and after about a mile reaches the hamlet of Beckstones. From here, pleasant walking along grassy paths (signed 'Torver Commons') leads to Coniston Water by way of the tiny tarns, Kelly Hall Tarn and Long Moss. The delightful stroll along the lakeside may be enhanced by the sight of a steam-driven iron boat *Gondola* as it chugs up and down. Look out for the remains of ancient 'bloomeries' where charcoal fuelled the smelting of iron ore, the high temperatures needed being achieved by the use of bellows.

An extract from an 1896 Furness Railway Map

Tour 9: The Tarn Hows Tour
Ambleside-Tarn Hows-Coniston-Elter Water-Clappersgate-Ambleside

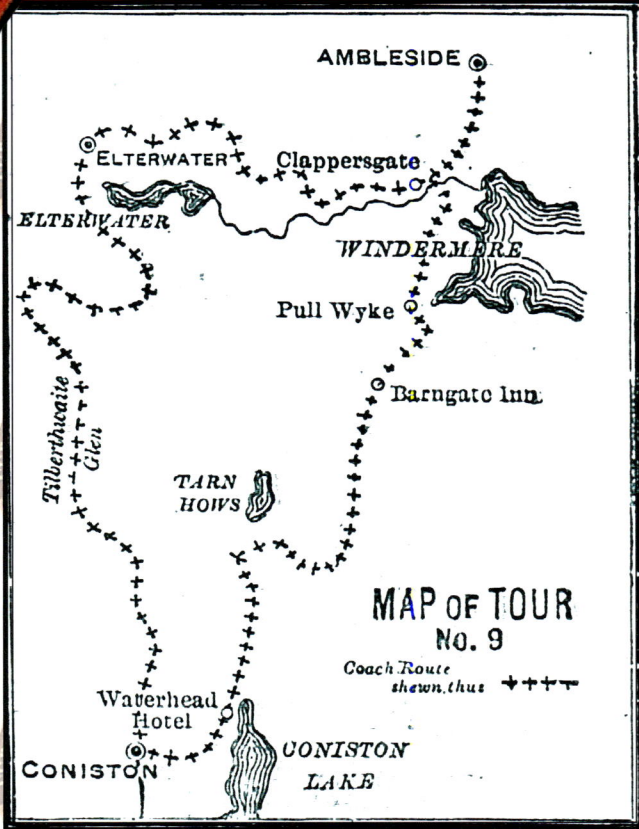

AMBLESIDE

ELTERWATER   Clappersgate

ELTERWATER

WINDERMERE

Pull Wyke

Barngate Inn

Tilberthwaite Glen

TARN HOWS

MAP OF TOUR No. 9

Coach Route shewn thus ✜✜✜

Waterhead Hotel

CONISTON   CONISTON LAKE

As mentioned in Tour 8 above, Tour 9 again did not include a Furness Railway rail or lake steamer element, but made up for this by visiting picturesque out-of-the-way locations that could be reached only by means of minor roads that passed through outstanding scenery.

As with Tour 8, Ambleside is a fine place to begin this journey. Following the same outward route along the A593 towards Coniston, turn left as before onto the B5286 at Clappersgate, which soon brings us near to **Pull Wyke Bay** on Windermere, a large bay that is a refuge for water birds and waders and bordered on its right-hand side by the headland of Brock Crag – although the badgers are not here, but in the woodland further back from the lake. Two becks flow into Pull Wyke Bay, and after crossing the second of these we turn right towards the inn now known as The Drunken Duck, formerly the Barngate Inn, a popular

inn and restaurant on the crossroads at Barngates, which features its own brewery.

A couple of miles further along this minor road, we come to the turning on the right for the popular beauty spot of **Tarn Hows**. The present-day tarn was created in the 19th century by joining three smaller tarns together and is now managed by the National Trust, which was gifted the estate by Beatrix Potter. Surrounded by woodland and offering splendid views of the Helvellyn range and the Langdale Pikes, its sheer beauty acts as a magnet for visitors who can enjoy the stunning setting from all angles, as a level and well-maintained footpath encircles the tarn providing an easy walk of about 1½ miles (2.5km). A welcome recent addition is a new building providing toilet facilities and public information displays under a 'green roof' of sedum to harmonise with its surroundings.

Leaving the idyllic setting of Tarn Hows, we continue along our route, rejoining the B5285 past the northern tip of Coniston Water to the village of **Coniston** itself. Here the journey could be broken by lunch at the Waterhead Hotel, whose beautiful grounds run down to the shore of Coniston Water and which offers a friendly welcome to its comfortable lounge bar, with stunning views over the lake and beyond. For more information about Coniston, see Tour 1, the Outer Circular Tour (page 99).

From Coniston take the A593 north towards Ambleside, following the valley of Yewdale Beck, then Tilberthwaite Glen. After about 4 miles (6.5km) a minor road on the left leads towards Little Langdale and Elter Water. Passing Colwith Force to our left and ignoring a left turn to Little Langdale, we continue towards the village

Above: **BARNGATES** The popular Drunken Duck inn and restaurant, close to the north-west end of Windermere.

Above and right: **TARN HOWS** The Lakeland Fells are reflected in the tranquil waters of Tarn Hows in its idyllic setting, seen here in October 1987.

of Langdale, passing Elter Water to our right. About half a mile (800m) further on turn right along the B5343 to join the A593 once, and turn left for our final run via Clappersgate back to Ambleside.

Right and below: **CONISTON** The Waterhead Hotel at Coniston offers visitors a superb outlook over the lake and surrounding hills, while its gardens with well-kept paths lead down to the jetty where the cruise boats put in.

Right: **COLWITH FORCE** on the River Brathay is especially impressive after heavy rain.

MAP OF TOUR No. 10

Stickle Pike 2303
Harrison Stickle 2401
Dungeon Ghyll Falls

Coach Route shewn thus ++++
Steamer ,, ,, -----

Wall End
New Hotel
Old Hotel
Blea Tarn
Gt. Langdale
Chapel Stile
Little Langdale
Colwith
ELTER WATER
Loughrigg Tarn
Red Bank
GRASMERE
GRASMERE LAKE
RYDAL WATER
RYDAL
AMBLESIDE
WINDERMERE LAKE
Pier
Waterhead Hotel

Tour 10: Round the Langdales and Dungeon Ghyll Tour
Ambleside-Elter Water-Blea Tarn-Dungeon Ghyll-Great Langdale-Red Bank-Grasmere-Rydal-Ambleside

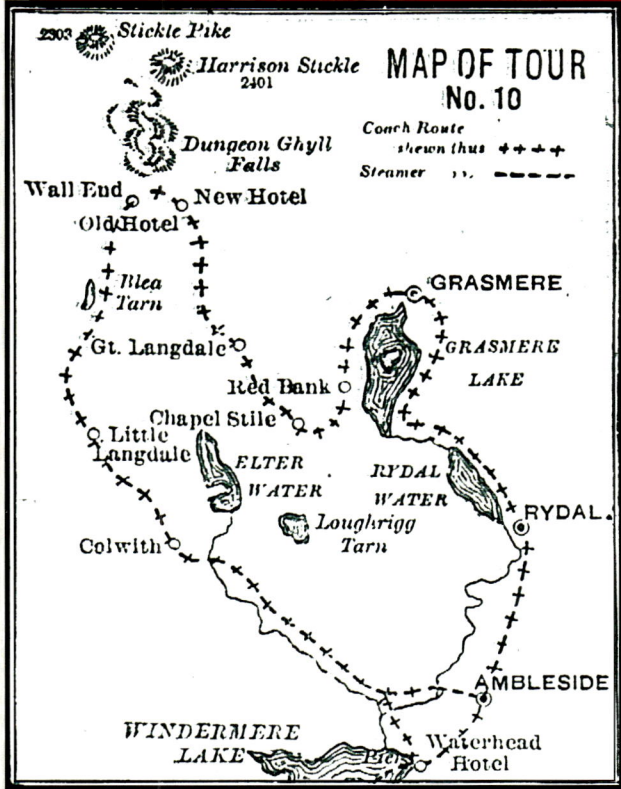

Ambleside is once again a convenient starting point for this circular tour, which like some earlier tours featured no railway component, but did offer the tourist the opportunity to take the lake steamer on Windermere from the pier at Waterhead. From here, the round trip down the lake to Bowness was a very pleasant way to spend a couple of hours on a sunny morning, gliding effortlessly through the stunning mountain scenery. The coach from Ambleside

AMBLESIDE's Waterhead Pier is a popular starting point for a cruise down Windermere.

would then carry the returning clients to visit the Langdale area before moving on to view the Falls at Dungeon Ghyll. They would then head south again around Grasmere before returning to Ambleside by way of Rydal.

The route today by car from Ambleside to the falls at **Colwith Force** is described in Tour 5 (see page 114). Colwith Force on the River Brathay drops from a height of about 12 metres in several stages, making an impressive cascade, especially after rain. For those of a more energetic disposition there is a very pleasant circular walk from Colwith Force which takes in Elter Water and Skelwith Force, a distance of less than 5 miles (8km). The area is managed by the National Trust and the walk is through woodland and riverside fields with the impressive falls providing an attractive bonus.

The River Brathay flows from the heights of Wrynose Pass, through Little Langdale Tarn and the valley of the same name, eventually emptying into Windermere. The area was once the centre of extensive copper and slate mining and some of the impressive but now disused workings can still be visited, with Cathedral Quarries and Greenburn Mine being the best-known and most frequented. For further details see www. visitcumbria.com/amb/cathedral-cave.

Continuing along the minor road westwards from Colwith Force past Little Langdale Tarn, then northwards to reach the larger **Blea Tarn**, located in a hanging valley between Great and Little Langdale. There is a car park here and an easy walk along a well-maintained trail around the tarn. It was designated an SSSI in 1989, one of several such sites in the area, emphasising the unique nature of this part of the Lake District.

Little more than a mile (1.6km) further on we come to the head of Great Langdale (often referred to simply as 'Langdale'), an area much loved by hikers, climbers and other outdoor enthusiasts, attracted by the impressive fells which ring the head of

Top left: **SKELWITH FORCE** The River Brathay cascades over Skelwith Force.

Left: **ELTER WATER** and the Langdale Pikes, as depicted on a Furness Railway postcard.

An extract from an 1896 Furness Railway Map

the valley. The Langdale Pikes offer spectacular views towards the 'high spots' of Harrison Stickle and Stickle Pike as well as the Dungeon Ghyll waterfall.

The most famous pub in the area is **The Old Dungeon Ghyll**, known to climbers and hikers as 'ODG', which distinguishes it from the New Dungeon Ghyll Hotel, built in 1862 lower down the valley. It features the Hikers Bar, which has a long association with climbing, while the Old Hotel has hosted many famous names over the years, notably Sir John Hunt – leader of the 1953 British Expedition to Mount Everest, the first successful attempt, when the summit was reached by Edmund Hillary and Tenzing Norgay – and

Above: **Nr SKELWITH FORCE T**he River Brathay near Skelwith Force. Slate mining is still carried out in the area and an impressive display of finished stone can be viewed at the nearby Kirkstone Works beside the B5343 at Skelwith Bridge.

Right: **BLEA TARN** in Langdale, from an FR postcard. *Ken Norman collection*

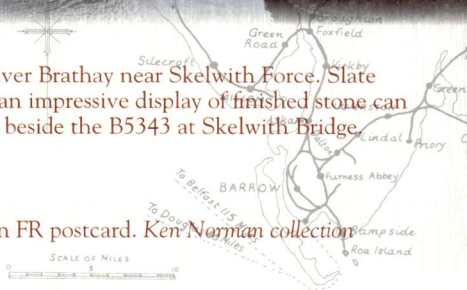

BLEA TARN, LANGDALE.   AMBLESIDE OR CONISTON STATIONS.

An extract from an 1896 Furness Railway Map

Left: **LITTLE LANGDALE TARN** from an FR postcard. *Ken Norman collection*

DUNGEON GHYLL FORCE, Langdale – an FR postcard of about 1906. *Ken Norman collection*

other members of his team including deputy leader Sir Charles Evans, Mike Westmacott, Tom Bourdillon and photographer Alf Gregory. More recently, Chris Bonnington and fellow climbers Joe Brown and Don Williams have frequented the famous bar. For the adventurous, a well-trodden path leads from the Stickle Ghyll car park at the Old Dungeon Ghyll up to Stickle Ghyll and its tarn, being just one of a series of classic walks featured in guides available from the ODG or through its website at www.odg.co.uk.

Heading east and south, follow what has become the B5343 towards Grasmere, the route taking us down Great Langdale through Chapel Stile, then turn left through Red Bank before circling the lake. The route from Red Bank around Grasmere and back to Ambleside via Rydal is described in Tour 5 (page 114).

described in Tour 5 (page 114).

An extract from an 1896 Furness Railway Map

Tour 11: The Ullswater Tour
Ambleside-Kirkstone Pass-Patterdale-Ullswater-Patterdale-Troutbeck-Ambleside

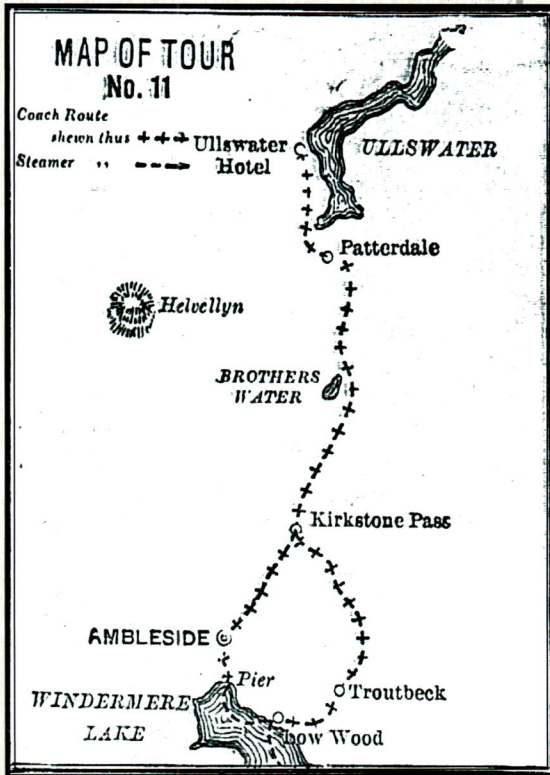

MAP OF TOUR No. 11

Coach Route
shewn thus +++
Steamer " - - -

ULLSWATER
Ullswater Hotel
Patterdale
Helvellyn
BROTHERS WATER
Kirkstone Pass
AMBLESIDE
Pier
Troutbeck
WINDERMERE LAKE
Low Wood

Tour 11 was another of the Furness Railway tours that did not feature the railway, but did include the company's Windermere steamer service. The suggested route was once again from the popular resort of Ambleside, travelling north by coach through the rugged scenery of Kirkstone Pass. After that, the route of what is now the A592 would take them north alongside Brothers Water to Patterdale at the southern end of Ullswater, before reaching their destination of the Ullswater Hotel beside the lake at Glenridding. The return journey would see them pass the Kirkstone Inn to follow the modern-day A592 down through the Vale of Troutbeck to Low Wood on Windermere. There the pier allowed connection with the Windermere steamer, whereupon the passengers could extend their journey by cruising down to Bowness and then back to Ambleside, or sail directly back to their starting point.

To take this tour by car today, we leave Ambleside by a minor road that branches right from the A591 to the north of the town and heads towards the Kirkstone Inn near the summit of the **Kirkstone Pass**, the highest pass in the Lake District. This road is known locally as 'The Struggle', and with gradients as testing as 1 in 4 on the approach to the inn it is not difficult to understand why.

KIRKSTONE PASS A sign warning drivers of the severity of the road ahead over the Lake District's highest pass.

KIRKSTONE PASS The scene in Kirkstone Pass, circa 1910, as horse-drawn carriages begin the ascent. Kirkstone is the Lake District's highest pass open to motor traffic, and connects Ambleside in the Rother Valley with Patterdale in the Ullswater Valley by means of the A592 road, in parts as steep as 1 in 4.

Near the top of the pass the road joins the A592; turn left past the summit and head towards Patterdale. We soon come upon the small lake of Brothers Water in the Hartsop Valley; our route runs close to the lake's eastern shore, while opposite the flank of Hartsop How rises steeply from the valley. The village of **Hartsop** is notable for having several 17th-century stone farm buildings and cottages. It is a popular starting point for hill-walkers visiting High Street and the Helvellyn range. The National Trust property, Hartsop Hall, lies on the far side of the valley from the village and dates from the 16th century. Lead mining was once carried out in the area and the remains of old workings can be discerned on the ridge of Hartsop Dodd, which overlooks the village from the east.

Further north we come to the village of **Patterdale** near the southern end of Ullswater. Popular with walkers for offering easy access to that favourite amongst the Lakeland peaks, Helvellyn, it is famed for a path, not for the faint-hearted, along the vertiginous Striding Edge. **Ullswater** is the Lake District's

Furness Railway. ULLSWATER. VIA LAKE SIDE STATION (WINDERMERE).

ULLSWATER from an FR postcard.

second largest lake at 7½ miles (12km) long, and we now travel along its western shore to our destination, the Ullswater Hotel at **Glenridding**, now called The Inn on the Lake.

The village is home to Ullswater Steamers, which began operations in 1859 and is still carrying passengers aboard its beautifully restored vessels between Glenridding and Pooley Bridge. A fuller description of Ullswater and Pooley Bridge will be found in Tour 15, the Six Lakes Circular Tour (page 143).

Returning south, we retrace our route along the A592 to Kirkstone Pass and remain on this road beyond the inn to follow the valley of the Trout Beck towards the village of the same name. At Town Head, turn right onto a minor road through High Green and Town End, then right again to Low Wood on Windermere. From here, the A591 hugs the eastern shore of Windermere as we travel back to Ambleside.

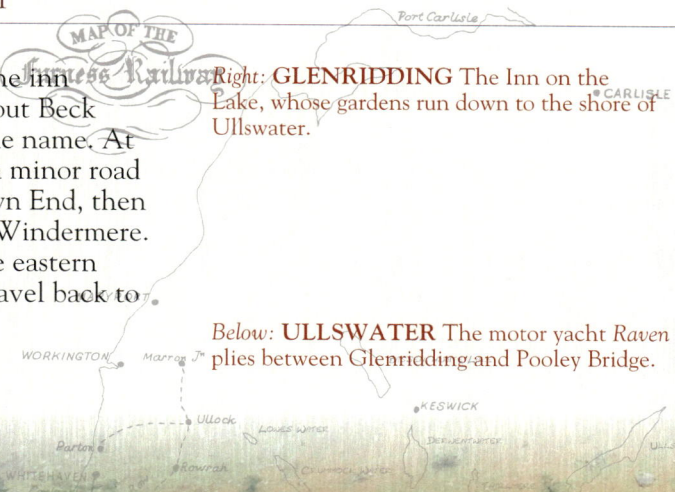

Right: **GLENRIDDING** The Inn on the Lake, whose gardens run down to the shore of Ullswater.

Below: **ULLSWATER** The motor yacht *Raven* plies between Glenridding and Pooley Bridge.

MAP OF TOUR No. 14

Great Gable
Wasdale Head Hotel
The Pikes
Scafell
Yewbarrow
Coach Route shewn thus ++++
Middle Fell
WASTWATER
The Screes
Wasdale Hall
Strands
Gosforth
Furness Railway
To Barrow
SEASCALE
From Whitehaven

Tour 14: The Wast Water Tour
Broughton-Seascale-Wast Water-Great Gable-Wast Water-Seascale-Broughton

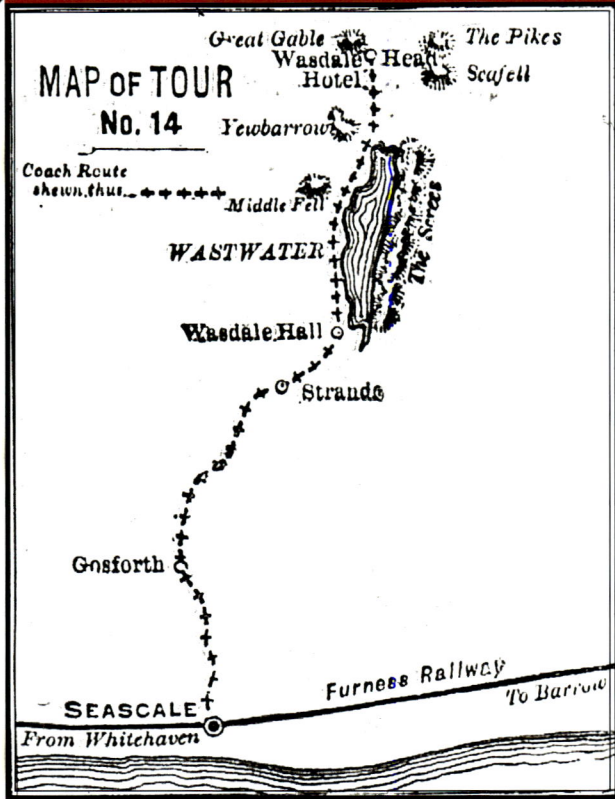

Although this tour might give the initial impression of having been merely a return coach trip from Seascale to Wasdale Head, in reality it offers far more than that.

To make the most of this excursion it is best to replicate the original railway journey. A suggested starting point therefore would be in the southern part of the National Park at **Broughton in Furness**, a small town close to the A595 road linking the Furness peninsula with the Irish Sea coast of West Cumbria. Broughton had a station on the Furness Railway's Coniston branch of 1859; see Tour 1, the Outer Circular Tour (page 99), for more details of the branch. There is a well-stocked Tourist Information Centre in the Square, and a number of pubs, cafes, shops and a Post Office are close at hand.

About 2 miles (3.2km) south-west of Broughton lies the coastal hamlet of **Foxfield**, with its station on the Cumbrian Coast line, which skirts the estuary of the River Duddon at Duddon Sands. The station became an important junction in the mid 19th century, being the point at which services for Broughton and Coniston connected with the FR main line between Barrow and Whitehaven. Today Foxfield is a 'request stop'

FURNESS RAILWAY,
Wastwater Circular Tour
Avl as per Advertisement

Whitehaven
TO
RAVENGLASS
& BACK

First Class

Not Transferable

FURNESS RAILWAY,
Wastwater Circular Tour
Rail & Coach

Ravenglass
TO
DALEGARTH
via N.G.Ry & MOTOR
& BACK To
RAVENGLASS
Avl as per Advertisement
See Over

A 1st Class ticket for Tour 14, The Wastwater Tour, which also included travel on the narrow-gauge Ravenglass & Eskdale Railway.

An extract from an 1896 Furness Railway Map

the village of Silecroft, and from there runs north, parallel with the railway, through Bootle, before coming to the estuary of the River Esk near Ravenglass – the headquarters of the narrow-gauge Ravenglass & Eskdale Railway – refer to Tour 13, the Five Lakes Circular Tour (page 53), for more information about this railway.

Beyond Ravenglass continue along the A595 to the village of Holmrook, where the B5344 branches off to the left to take us through Drigg to the coast at **Seascale**. With the arrival of the Furness Railway Seascale became popular with Victorian tourists attracted by its fine beach, complete with bathing machines, and of course it served as an excellent base from which to explore the valleys of the western Lake District.

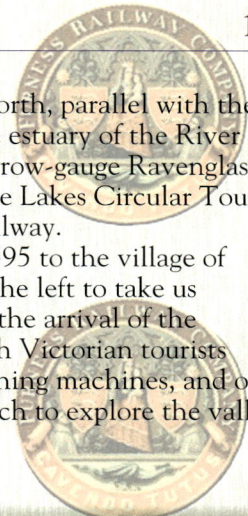

Above: **FOXFIELD** station, complete with signal box and water tower, is seen in April 2014. The platforms afford splendid views across the Duddon Sands.

Right: Direct Rail Services Class 37s Nos 37603 and 37423 take their train of low-level nuclear waste flasks along the Cumbrian Coast line from the reprocessing plant at Sellafield on 23 October 2012.

on this much-used line, whose regular passenger traffic is supplemented by freight services operated by DRS to and from the Sellafield Nuclear Reprocessing Plant.

The railway runs close by the coast, offering great views across Duddon Sands, an area designated as an SSSI and a Special Protection Area under the European Union Directive on the Conservation of Wild Birds. This internationally recognised haven for seabirds and waders can also be appreciated by road, by taking the A5093 towards Millom, which branches from the A595 about 5 miles (8km) west of Broughton in Furness. This road eventually loops back to rejoin the A595 just beyond

An extract from an 1896 Furness Railway Map

Leave Seascale along the B5344 to Gosforth, then cross the A595 and take the minor road opposite towards **Wast Water**, England's deepest lake. On reaching the lake the road hugs its north-western shore, and as we proceed up Wasdale we enter an area surrounded by some of the highest mountains in England. To our left we are overlooked initially by Middle Fell, with its rugged terrain, hostile crags and tumbled boulders.

Almost immediately this is followed by the high narrow ridge of Yewbarrow, aptly described as having the shape of an upturned boat. Coming to the end of the lake, the road terminates at Wasdale Head where we find the Wasdale Head Inn, which

Left: **WAST WATER** The narrow road beside the lake provides ample opportunities to stop and admire the fine scenery.

describes itself as 'the birthplace of British rock climbing'. Billed as the only hotel in Wasdale Valley, it is uniquely situated at the foot of Scafell Pike and Great Gable, whose stunning peaks make this a climber's Mecca.

As there is but one road up through Wasdale, our return route must involve us retracing our journey, but this reveals a whole new vista as we head south-west along the lake shore. Across the water we can see the boulder-strewn craggy fell side known as The Screes, formed as a result of freeze-thaw weathering and erosion of the rock from the fells to

WASTWATER AND SCAWFELL.

SEASCALE STATION.

Furness Railway.   WASTWATER.   SEASCALE STATION.

Above: **WAST WATER** portrayed on an FR postcard.
Left: **WAST WATER** 'Wastwater and Scawfell', from a postcard by Raphael Tuck & Sons Ltd, Series 5, produced for the Furness Railway in about 1900.

An extract from an 1896 Furness Railway Map

An extract from an 1896 Furness Railway Map

the east. Towards the southern end of the lake is Wasdale Hall, a half-timbered house owned by the National Trust dating back to 1829. Retaining many of its original features and offering stunning views over the lake and surrounding hills, it is now the home of the Wastwater Youth Hostel.

On arriving back at Gosforth, follow the A595 back to our starting point at Broughton in Furness.

Left: **WASDALE HEAD** Dwarfed by the bulk of the surrounding fells, the Wasdale Head Inn is perfectly situated to provide a base from which to explore England's deepest lake and highest mountains.

Below left: **WASDALE HEAD** The church of St Olaf, Wasdalehead, seen here on a postcard by Raphael Tuck & Sons, Furness Railway Series 5, circa 1910, is reputed to be the smallest church in England, with roof beams that came from a Viking longship. It is thought to be more than 1,000 years old and is now a Grade II listed building. It is kept open to visitors during the daytime.

Below: **WASDALE HEAD** The church of St Olaf photographed some 93 years later in April 2003. *J. Townsend*

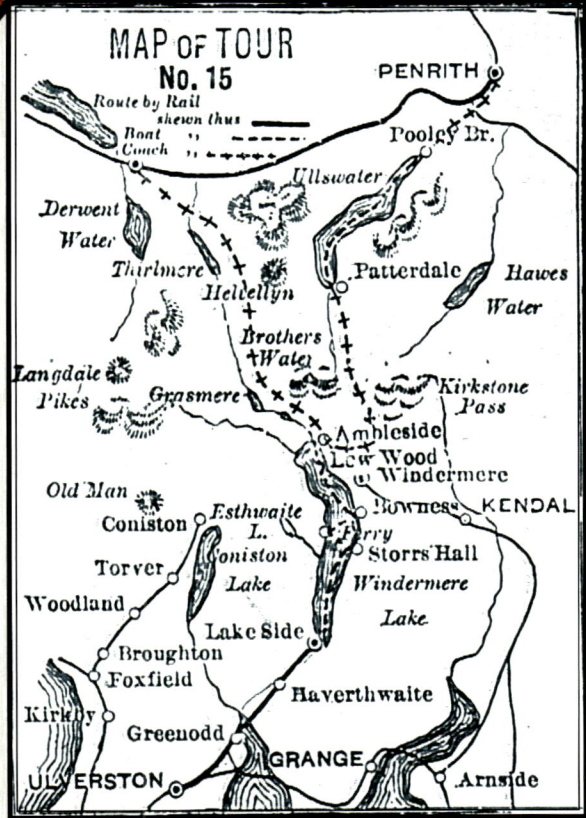

MAP OF TOUR
No. 15

Route by Rail
shewn thus
Boat
Coach

PENRITH
Pooley Br.
Ullswater
Derwent Water
Thirlmere
Helvellyn
Patterdale
Hawes Water
Brothers Water
Langdale Pikes
Grasmere
Kirkstone Pass
Ambleside
Low Wood
Windermere
Old Man
Esthwaite L.
Bowness
KENDAL
Coniston
Ferry
Storrs Hall
Torver
Coniston Lake
Windermere Lake
Woodland
Lake Side
Broughton
Foxfield
Haverthwaite
Kirkby
Greenodd
ULVERSTON
GRANGE
Arnside

SCALE OF MILES
0   5   10

Tour 15: The Six Lakes Circular Tour

Ulverston-Haverthwaite-Ambleside-Thirlmere-Keswick-Pooley Bridge-Ullswater-Patterdale-Kirkstone Pass-Ambleside-Lakeside-Haverthwaite-Ulverston

Alfred Aslett, Secretary and General Manager of the Furness Railway, is regarded as the man responsible for the transformation of the company from a struggling industrial operation into a successful and expanding railway empire, built very largely around his insistence that its future prosperity depended upon tourism, and what better location than the Lake District to develop and promote this policy? His Six Lakes Circular Tour is widely regarded as the crowning glory of the ambitious programme that he introduced, taking participants on a wide-ranging journey through stunning scenery, visiting Windermere, Rydal, Grasmere, Thirlmere, Derwentwater and Ullswater as they travelled in comfort by rail, charabanc and lake steamer.

This extract from *The Illustrated Guide to the Resorts of the Furness Railway*, published by Holmes of Ulverston in 1900, explains to the would-be tourist what joys lay ahead:

'The excursion goes by rail, say from Furness Abbey to the Company's Lake Side station on Windermere, thence by their steam yacht the whole reach of the lake to Ambleside, then by coach to Ullswater, where another steam yacht is in readiness to carry him to Pooley Bridge, after showing him the charms of the "English Lucerne". From this landing he continues his course by coach to Penrith, going by rail (via the London & North Western) to Keswick, and returning to Ambleside via Thirlmere, Grasmere and Rydal, by coach, where the Company's steam yacht again receives him and transfers him to the train at the foot of the lake, by which he returns to Furness Abbey.'

FURNESS ABBEY In FR days one of the starting points for this tour was Furness Abbey station, close to the ruins of the great monastery, seen here from Abbots Wood.

Today's public transport links in the Lake District cannot duplicate the carefully coordinated route put in place by Alfred Aslett, but it can be followed by car, and of course the lake cruises on Windermere and Ullswater are still in operation. Much of this extensive tour is described in detail elsewhere, as some of its components make up sections of other Furness Railway shorter excursions. Reference will be made to these earlier tours as appropriate.

For the sake of simplicity and to avoid an unnecessary drive, it is suggested that this tour

A coach journey along the shore of Ullswater circa 1900, passing Stybarrow Crag on what is now the A592 towards Pooley Bridge.

should start and end at the charming and historic market town of **Ulverston**, just north of Morecambe Bay. The first section takes us to the southern tip of Windermere at Newby Bridge, by way of the A590 through Greenodd and Haverthwaite, then on from Newby Bridge along the eastern shore of Windermere following the A592 to the popular tourist destination of **Ambleside**; this route is detailed in Tour 1, the Outer Circular Tour (page 99).

Our route from Ambleside takes us to the head of the Kirkstone Pass, as described in Tour 11, the Ullswater Tour (page 135), by way of a minor road from the town that joins the A592 near the top of the pass, and continues north past Brothers Water to Patterdale, at the foot of Ullswater. Participants on the Furness Railway tour would then have boarded the Ullswater steamer at Glenridding Pier for the next stage of the journey up the lake. **Glenridding** is home to Ullswater Steamers. This company, founded

Furness Railway. NEWBY BRIDGE (Windermere). LAKE SIDE STATION.

NEWBY BRIDGE from an FR postcard, circa 1900.

ULLSWATER Looking along Ullswater towards Glenridding.

in 1855 as the Ullswater Steam Navigation Company, operated the paddle steamer *Enterprise*, but unfortunately she had to be replaced as her paddles repeatedly became choked by weed. Her successor, the motor yacht *Lady of the Lake*, launched in 1877, carried mail, passengers and provisions around the lake for what was by then called the Ullswater Navigation & Transit Company Limited, as well as slate and lead from the mines near Glenridding. Together with the MY *Raven*, launched in 1889, she

was converted to run on diesel oil and both vessels have been in service ever since. MY *Lady of the Lake* is believed to be the oldest working passenger vessel in the world.

Our journey continues north along the wonderfully scenic A592 as it hugs the shore of Ullswater, with the sweeping grassy slopes of Stybarrow Dodd away to our left, and passing the famous Aira Force waterfall near the junction with the A5091. At the head of the lake we pass the small village of **Pooley Bridge**, and a little further on a minor road on the left leads to Dacre and the A66. However, the Furness Railway

tour participants would have travelled on to the market town of Penrith, and this is well worth visiting today, so continue on the A592 until it joins the A66, and turn right.

Penrith has considerable historical railway interest. Situated in the luscious Eden Valley, Penrith station on the West Coast Main Line south of Carlisle is also known as 'Penrith North Lakes'. Built by the Lancaster & Carlisle Railway and opened in 1846, it was once a busy

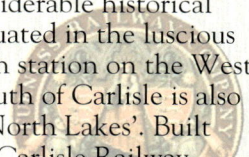

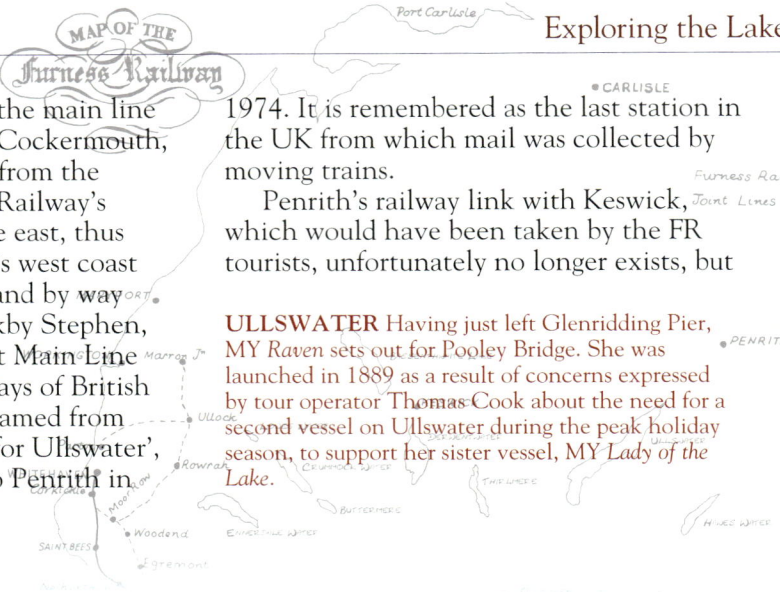

junction, being not only on the main line but also the terminus of the Cockermouth, Keswick & Penrith Railway from the west and the North Eastern Railway's Eden Valley branch from the east, thus serving to connect Cumbria's west coast with the North East of England by way of the Stainmore line at Kirkby Stephen, and further to the East Coast Main Line at Darlington. In the early days of British Railways the station was renamed from simply 'Penrith' to 'Penrith for Ullswater', though the name reverted to Penrith in 1974. It is remembered as the last station in the UK from which mail was collected by moving trains.

Penrith's railway link with Keswick, which would have been taken by the FR tourists, unfortunately no longer exists, but

ULLSWATER Having just left Glenridding Pier, MY *Raven* sets out for Pooley Bridge. She was launched in 1889 as a result of concerns expressed by tour operator Thomas Cook about the need for a second vessel on Ullswater during the peak holiday season, to support her sister vessel, MY *Lady of the Lake*.

the route is followed today by the A66 road, and this section of our journey is described in Tour 13, The Five Lakes Circular Tour (page 53). In an article for *The Railway Magazine* in February 1985, entitled 'Lakeland Tribulations – the lack of lines in the Lake District', author Martin Bairstow questioned the short-sighted closure of lines penetrating the interior of the Lake District. These included the Cockermouth, Keswick & Penrith, (especially the Keswick-Penrith section), further south the Plumpton Junction to Haverthwaite line (which could have made the Lakeside & Haverthwaite Railway among the country's leading preservation projects), and the Coniston branch. He asked why the replacement bus connections never appeared in BR timetables, an omission that exacerbated the problems for locals and visitors alike resulting from the closure of the rail links to the region's interior.

Left: **AIRA FORCE** The impressive falls tumble down towards Ullswater from Gowbarrow Fell. The falls are easily accessible from the road along the lake, being on the edge of the former medieval deer park of Gowbarrow Park, now owned by the National Trust, close to the point where the A5091 from Troutbeck reaches the lake to meet the A592.

Right: **PENRITH** Your author at Penrith station in 1971, before 'for Ullswater' was removed from the name.

Above: **PENRITH** On 10 May 2014 a First TransPennine Express service from Manchester to Edinburgh arrives at Penrith station in the form of Class 350/4 EMU No 350406. Ten of these sets, with a top speed of 110mph (177kmh), were built during 2013-14 and feature an 'InterCity'-style layout.

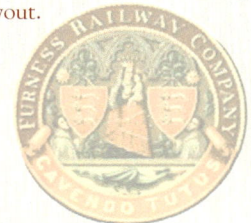

An extract from an 1896 Furness Railway Map

Take the A66 west to the tourist 'hot-spot' of Keswick, then head south along the A591 beside the lofty peak of Helvellyn, near Thirlmere, via Ambleside to Windermere, then the A592 through Bowness to Newby Bridge, and finally the A590 to our starting point of Ulverston, as detailed in Tour 12, the Derwentwater (Keswick) Tour (page 45).

Above: **PENRITH** Opposite the station are the ruins of Penrith Castle, built between 1399 and 1470 as part of the English defences against raiders from Scotland. The castle was once also owned by the Lancaster & Carlisle Railway Company, though it later passed into the care of Penrith Urban District Council and is now maintained by English Heritage.

Above right and right: **PENRITH** Next to the Castle stands the imposing and recently refurbished Station Hotel, still retaining much of railway interest, including its sign above the entrance.

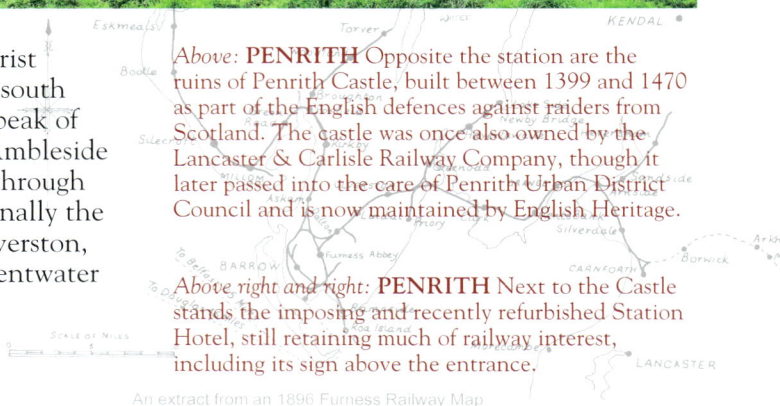

An extract from an 1896 Furness Railway Map

MAP OF TOUR
NO. 16

Route by Coach
shewn thus + + +

SEATHWAITE
TARN

Seathwaite
Church

Newfield

Hall Dunnerdale

Kirkhouse

Ulpha

Whineray
Ground

Woodland

Duddon Bridge

Broughton

Foxfield

R. Duddon

Duddon Sands

An extract from an 1896 Furness Railway Map

Tour 16: The Duddon Valley Tour
Ulverston-Foxfield-Broughton-Duddon Bridge-Kirkhouse-Dunnerdale Hall-Newfield-Kirkhouse-Duddon Bridge-Broughton-Foxfield-Ulverston

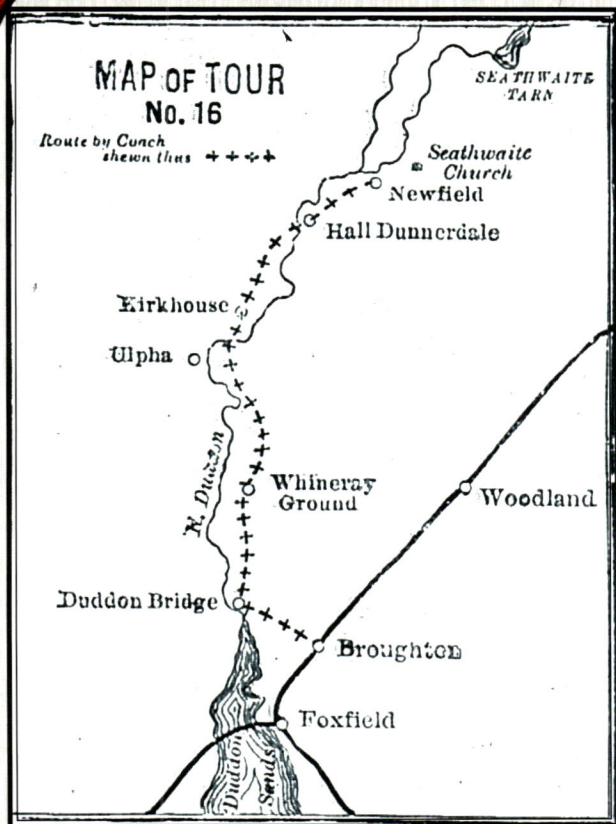

In Furness Railway days this tour involved first a rail journey from Barrow-in-Furness or perhaps Ulverston along the main line to the small station at Foxfield, where the Coniston branch was taken as far as Broughton in Furness. From this point, passengers would transfer to a coach for their onward journey up the Duddon Valley. Today, the village of Foxfield on the Duddon Estuary retains its station, though now only as a 'request stop' on the Cumbrian Coast line, and the Coniston branch was closed to passenger trains in 1958 and to goods traffic four years later.

The beautiful **Duddon Estuary** is designated an SSSI and a Special Protection Area under the EU Birds Directive, being internationally important not only for its wintering and breeding bird populations, but also because of its other endangered fauna and its special geological features. It is home to natterjack toads, an impressive 19 species of butterfly, more than 270 plant species, including the rare bee orchid, and of course a wealth of estuary birds. The nearby slag banks are important nesting sites for large colonies of sandwich, common, little and Arctic tern, while Hodbarrow Point, near Millom, is noted for red-breasted merganser, eider and goldeneye. There is an RSPB hide accessible along the main trail (a firm surface suitable for pushchairs and wheelchairs) about 1½ miles (2.3km) from the car park at Mainsgate Road. For more information, visit www.rspb.org.uk/reserves/guide/h/hodbarrow.

The area sprang to importance with the establishment of the Duddon Bridge Iron Furnace in 1736, producing pig iron from imported haematite brought up the Duddon by boat. This furnace ceased operations in 1867, but its remains provide one of the best surviving examples of a charcoal-fired blast furnace in Britain. Further discoveries of haematite deposits in the area led to the construction of other blast furnaces associated with the new mines, which together with the railway brought an influx of new labour and prosperity to the beautiful Duddon Valley.

Today's tour by car begins beside the estuary at Foxfield and we take the A595 towards Millom, but turn right after a short distance onto a minor road leading to the small town of **Broughton in Furness**, which has an attractive Georgian Market Square and obelisk, with a Tourist Information Centre in the Town Hall, the former Market Hall, in the Square.

Returning to the A595 and travelling west, we soon come to **Duddon Bridge** across the River Duddon, which historically formed the boundary between the counties of Lancashire and Cumberland (since local government reorganisation in 1974 the Duddon has been in the county of Cumbria). It is frequented by canoeists and also by anglers in search of salmon. William Wordsworth wrote extensively about the Duddon, a river he knew and loved, penning a series of sonnets between 1804 and 1820. In Sonnet 1 he wrote:

'All hail, ye mountains! Hail, thou morning light!
Better to breathe at large on this aery height
Than toil in needless sleep from dream to dream;
Pure flow the verse, pure, vigorous, free, and bright,
For Duddon, long-loved Duddon, is my theme!'

Having visited Duddon Bridge, take the turn to the north on the Broughton side of the bridge towards Ulpha. This minor road takes us up through **Dunnerdale**, with the Dunnerdale Fells rising steeply on our right,

BROUGHTON TOWER stands on the site of the former castle.

An extract from an 1896 Furness Railway Map

ULPHA From the tiny village of Ulpha, the lovely valley of Dunnerdale unfolds before you.

DUDDON BRIDGE, where the A595 trunk road around the estuary between Broughton in Furness and Millom crosses the river.

DUDDON FURNACE Travelling from Foxfield, Duddon Furnace is located near Duddon Bridge. Cross the bridge and turn immediately right; the entrance to the furnace area is 100 metres on the left.

known for the classic 'Fell Race' contested here annually in November. Continuing along this lovely valley we come to Hall Dunnerdale, a scattering of typical Lake District stone cottages, some of which have been 'upgraded' to provide accommodation for holidaymakers who visit this secluded landscape.

A little further up the valley beyond Ulpha is the village of **Seathwaite,** and beyond is Seathwaite Tarn, which was enlarged by the construction of a dam in 1904 to create a reservoir Nearby is Birks Bridge, a Grade 2 listed structure built in the 19th century and made of stone rubble. It has drainage channels in the parapets and voussoirs (drainage holes) to allow flood water to pass through. The gorge below has

An extract from an 1896 Furness Railway Map

Above: **DUNNERDALE** The sparkling waters of the River Duddon flow down the valley towards the sea at Duddon Sands.

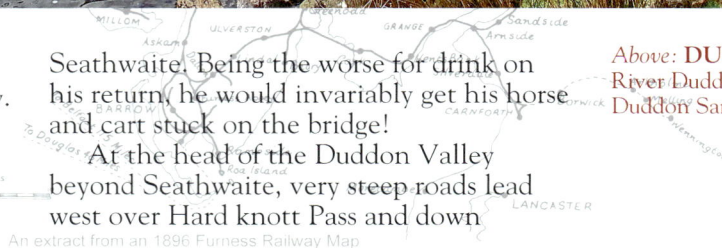

been smoothed by the constant passage of the river, often very fierce when in full flow. The name comes from the birch trees that can be found around here, hence Birch or 'Birks' Bridge. An old yarn tells of a local who liked to frequent the Newfield Inn in Seathwaite. Being the worse for drink on his return, he would invariably get his horse and cart stuck on the bridge!

At the head of the Duddon Valley beyond Seathwaite, very steep roads lead west over Hard knott Pass and down

An extract from an 1896 Furness Railway Map

Above: **DUNNERDALE** The road through Dunnerdale provides access to a region of unspoilt natural beauty.

Above right: **DUNNERDALE** The charming valley surrounded by its fells leads us on to the high passes at its head.

Right: **SEATHWAITE TARN** in the Duddon Valley, 'Barrow Water Supply' according to this FR postcard view.

DUDDON VALLEY: SEATHWAITE TARN (BARROW WATER SUPPLY). E.F.CUGHTON STATION.

through Eskdale, and east over Wrynose Pass to Langdale. As might be expected, Dunnerdale is popular with walkers and climbers keen to experience the hills and valleys, especially the nearby Coniston Fells. Consequently the villages in the valley feature well-known pubs that pride themselves in catering to the needs of these explorers.

Unless the high roads out of the top of the valley are to be explored, the return journey involves retracing our route, as the FR travellers did, following the river back to its estuary at Duddon Sands.

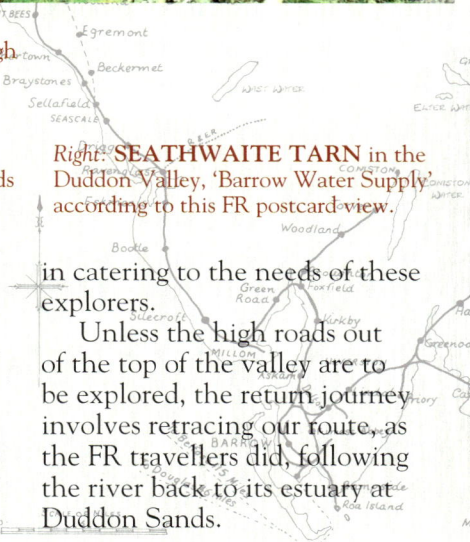

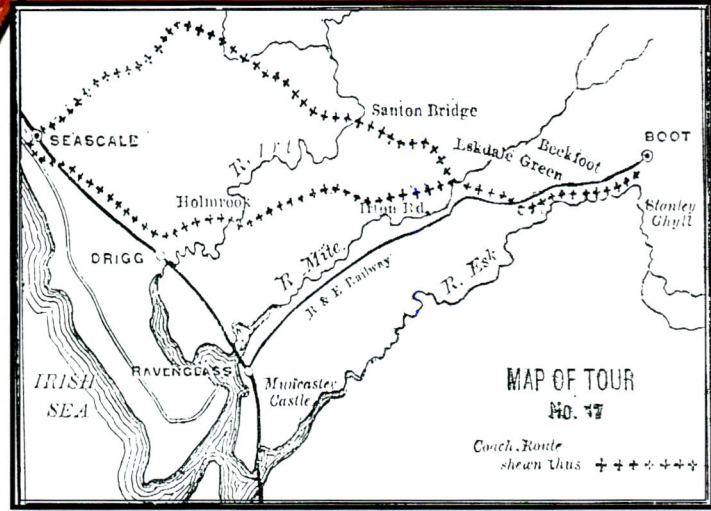

Map of the Furness Railway

MAP OF TOUR No. 17

Coach Route shown thus ++++++

Tour 17: The Three Valleys Tour
Seascale-Gosforth-Santon Bridge-Irton Road-Eskdale Green-Boot-Holmrook-Seascale

For the Furness Railway tourist this tour would begin with a journey by rail along the main line from Barrow-in-Furness, skirting the estuary of the River Duddon at Duddon Sands, then on along the beautiful Irish Sea coast to the village of Seascale. Transferring to a coach, the tour continued as a circular route by way of Gosforth to Santon Bridge in the Irt Valley, then across the valley of the River Mite and up into Eskdale to the village of Boot, near the terminus of the Ravenglass & Eskdale Railway. From Boot the route then returned to the Mite Valley before crossing and heading for Holmrook, in the Irt Valley. After Holmrook the coach would return to Seascale for the rail journey back down the coast.

Today, **Seascale** is a suitable starting point for what is now a circular tour. Promoted in the Victorian era as an up and coming holiday destination with miles of fine beaches and served by the new Furness Railway line form Barrow, the dream never quite materialised.

Left and opposite top: **SEASCALE** station overlooks the sandy beach with its wooden jetty and the fort.

It was not until after the Second World War, when the huge building programme at the former Royal Ordnance Factory at Sellafield a few miles away created the Windscale and Calder Hall nuclear site, later to become the Sellafield Nuclear Reprocessing Plant, that Seascale expanded as its dormitory community.

The seafront fort and the reinstated wooden jetty are popular with visitors and locals alike, while the nearby nature reserves of Drigg Dunes and Hallsenna Moor are nationally important havens for wildlife. At the railway station, the listed Victorian water tower built by the Furness Railway is a prominent feature, while the adjacent engine shed is now a sports hall.

We leave Seascale by the B5344 towards the small village of **Gosforth**, where St Mary's Church houses a collection of Norse

Right: **SEASCALE** A creative development sees the former engine shed next to the station in use as a sports hall, with the former water tower standing alongside.

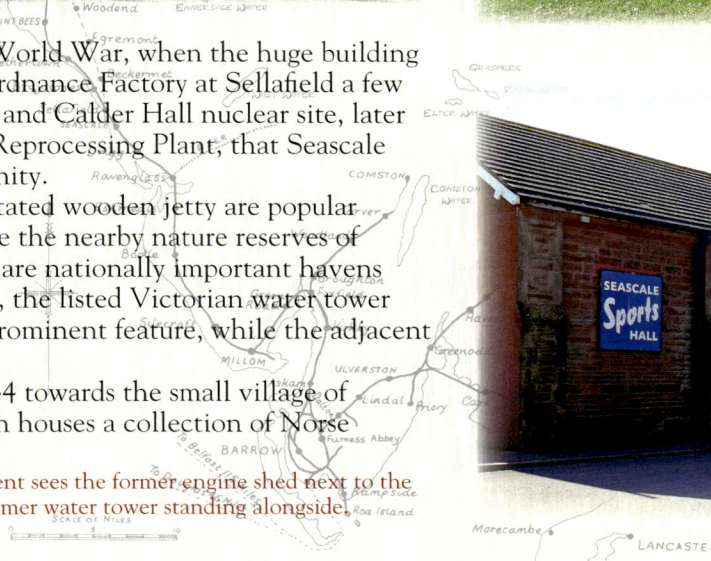

artefacts including the Gosforth Cross, reputed to be the tallest and oldest Viking Cross in England.

From Gosforth we take a minor road past Bolton Hall in the direction of the picturesque village of **Santon Bridge** on the River Irt, which is the outflow from Wast Water. Continuing across the valley below Irton Fell, we enter the adjacent valley of the River Mite, which rises on Tongue Moor in the Eskdale Fells near Burnmoor Tarn. After crossing the river, we come upon Irton Road, a station on the narrow-gauge Ravenglass & Eskdale Railway. In the grounds of the church of St Paul at **Irton** stands the Celtic Cross, erected here in the early 9th century at the crossing of four ancient tracks. The Irton Cross, as it is usually known, is held to be one of the most important in Cumbria, standing 3 metres high and still resting on its original socket stone. The church itself has an impressive collection of Victorian stained glass.

We now follow the road that parallels the railway eastwards through Eskdale Green and up the Esk Valley to the village of **Boot**, at the end of the line – see Tour 13, the Five Lakes Circular Tour (page 53), for further details of this area. The Ravenglass & Eskdale Railway's history is a fascinating story of the triumph of endurance over adversity, and time spent exploring around the line is rewarding. For more information visit www.ravenglass-railway.co.uk.

The village of **Eskdale Green** would make a very pleasant lunch location on our return journey eastwards, crossing the River Mite then turning left to head towards

Above: **GOSFORTH** The Gosforth Cross outside the Parish Church of St Mary.

Above and right: **IRTON** St Paul's Church at Irton, and the Irton Cross.

An extract from an 1896 Furness Railway Map

Left: DALEGARTH (BOOT)
The recently improved and extended station buildings at Dalegarth, the terminus of the Ravenglass & Eskdale Railway at Boot, offer excellent facilities to visitors.

Right: BECKFOOT The R&ER's 0-8-2 loco *River Irt* takes its train through Beckfoot station, just down the line from the terminus at Dalegarth (for Boot). Built in 1894, she is believed to be the oldest working 15-inch-gauge locomotive in the world.

Left: IRTON ROAD The railway's 2005-built B-B diesel-hydraulic loco *Douglas Ferreira* heads up the line from Ravenglass, passing through Irton Road station. Named after a former General Manager of the railway between 1961 and 1994, she is resplendent in the Indian Red livery of the Furness Railway.

Holmrook on the River Irt. Turn right onto the A595 into the village, then turn left to follow the minor road back to our starting point at Seascale.

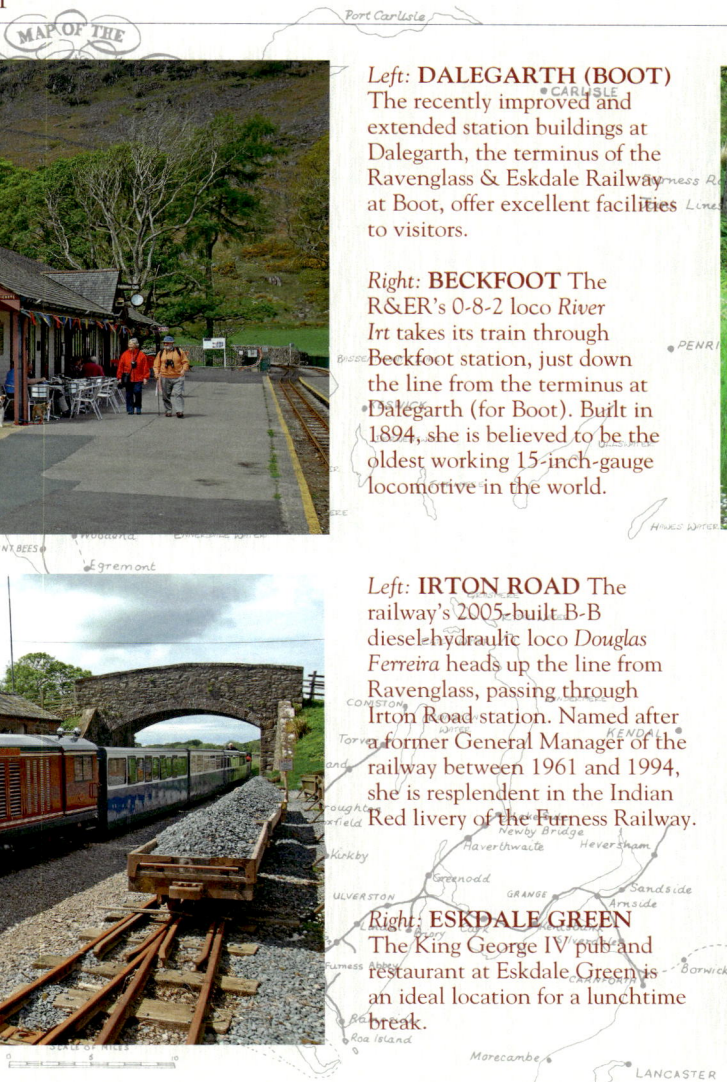

Right: ESKDALE GREEN The King George IV pub and restaurant at Eskdale Green is an ideal location for a lunchtime break.

Index

Aira Force 145, 146
Ambleside 12, 13, 38, 46, 118, 121, 122, 125, 128, 132, 135, 144; Pier (Waterhead) 39, 54, 114, 131
Armathwaite 57, 58
Arnside 10, 21-23; Area of Outstanding Natural Beauty 22; Arnside Knott 22; pier 22; viaduct 21, 22
Ashness 51, 52
Askam 101, 102, 109
Aslett, Alfred 12, 14, 41, 82, 97, 143-44

Backbarrow 30; dye works 30-32; ironworks 11, 29, 30, 32
Barngates 128, 129
Barrow, Sir John 99
Barrow Haematite Steel Co 11, 12
Barrow-in-Furness 8, 10, 21, 74, 101, 108; Dock Museum 102-03; steelworks 8, 13, 35, 41
Bassenthwaite Lake 56, 57
Beckstones 127
Birks Bridge 151-52
Blea Tarn 132, 133
Blelham Tarn 125, 126
Boot 66, 156
Bootle 71, 139
Borrowdale 119
Bowness-on-Windermere 12, 35, 36, 88

Braithwaite 55
Brantwood 124
Brathay, river 115, 116, 132, 133
Brockhole, Lake District Visitor Centre 114
Brothers Water 136, 144
Broughton in Furness 9, 43, 74, 78, 100, 109, 138, 150
Broughton Moor RNAD 60
Burlington, William, Earl of 9
Burneside 36, 37

Calder Abbey 80, 81, 144
Calder Bridge 80
Campbell, Donald 41, 43
Car Bells 51
Cark & Cartmel station 24, 93, 94
Carnforth 19-20, 36; Brief Encounter film 20; loco shed 20; Steamtown 19, 72; train service 21
Cartmel 94-95; Priory 13, 24, 92, 94
Castlerigg stone circle 49, 51
Cleator & Workington Junction Railway 60, 62, 84
Cleator Moor 81, 84
Coal mining 55, 60-61
Coast to Coast (C2C) Cycleway 82, 83, 84
Cockermouth 57
Cockermouth & Workington Railway 55, 58, 81

Cockermouth, Keswick & Penrith Railway 13, 51, 55, 56, 74, 77, 146, 147
Cold Fell 81
Colwith Force 115, 116, 129, 130, 132
Conishead Priory 28, 29
Coniston 10, 41, 42-43, 100, 110, 111, 112, 113, 121, 122-23, 126, 127, 129, 153; Hall 123, 124; Waterhead Hotel 129, 130 see also 'Old Man of Coniston'
Coniston Launch Co 40
Coniston Railway 11, 42-43, 100-01, 109, 110, 112, 147
Coniston Water 12, 17, 40, 41, 110, 112
Cook, Henry 12, 41
Copper mining 10, 40, 42, 100, 109, 110, 123, 132
Crayke, river 40
Cumbria Coastal Way 27
'Cumbrian Coast Express' train 87
Cumbrian Coast railway line 60, 65, 68, 86, 87, 138
Dalegarth 68, 69, 157; Hall 67 see also Boot
Dalton-in-Furness 9, 104, 106, 108
Derwent Water 49, 50, 52
Devonshire, Earls/Dukes of 9, 95
Dodd Wood 57
Dollywaggon Pike 48

Drigg 65-66, 139, 155
Duddon, river and estuary 72, 73, 138, 149, 150; viaduct 73
Duddon Bridge 149-51
Duddon Sands 72-73, 106, 138, 139
Dungeon Ghyll and Force 133-34
Dunmail Raise 48, 118, 120
Dunnerdale 150-51, 152-53

Egremont 81; Castle 80-81
Elter Water 115, 121, 122, 126, 129, 130, 132
Embleton 57
Ennerdale Bridge and Water 64, 85
Eskdale 66, 67, 69, 153
Eskdale Green 66, 156, 157
Eskmeals 70-71
Esthwaite Water 89, 90

Far Sawrey 88, 91; Hill Top House 89
Ferry Nab, Windermere 88, 89
Foxfield 42, 73, 100, 109, 122, 138-39, 150
Friar's Crag 51
Furness & Lancaster & Carlisle Union Railway 23
Furness Abbey 9, 10, 26, 74, 80, 101, 103-05; Hotel 105, 119
Furness Railway 8-11, 12, 26, 39, 40-41, 42, 66, 82, 92, 96, 101, 110
Furness Railway Illustrated Guides 16-17

Glenridding 136, 137, 144-45, 146
Gosforth 79, 155-56
Gowan, river 37
Gowbarrow Park 147
Grange-over-Sands 10, 21, 24-26, 92
Grasmere 46, 47-48, 116-17, 118, 121
Great Gable 79, 141
Greenodd 10, 12, 29, 39-40, 96, 97, 113, 123
Greta Gorge 74
Grizedale Forest 90

Haig Colliery, Whitehaven 61-62, 63
Hard Knott Pass 69, 152
Hartsop 136
Haverthwaite 11, 24, 29, 31, 39, 96
Hawkshead 89, 90, 113
Helm Crag 48, 116
Helvellyn 49, 91, 119, 120, 128, 136, 148
High Raise 118
Hincaster Junction 23, 24
Hindpool Steel Works 8
Hodbarrow 71, 72, 73, 149
Holker Hall 10, 13, 95
Holme Fell 112
Holmrook 139, 157

Iron ore 24, 29, 55, 58, 59, 66, 67, 71, 102

Irt, river 156, 157
Irton 156; Irton Road station 157

Kelly Hall Tarn 127
Kendal 36, 37
Kendal & Windermere Railway 36, 74, 97
Kent, river and estuary 21, 23, 24, 37; viaduct 24
Kents Bank 24, 26, 27
Keswick 49, 51, 54, 56, 74
Kirkby-in-Furness 9
Kirkstone Pass 135-36, 144

Ladysmith Colliery, Whitehaven 61
Lake Bank (Coniston Water) 40, 41, 113
Lake District National Park 57, 66, 74
Lakeland Motor Museum 31
Lakes Aquarium 33, 96, 98
'Lakes Express' train 55
Lakeside & Haverthwaite Railway 24, 29, 39, 54, 72, 96, 147
Lakeside, Windermere 11, 12, 29, 32-33, 39, 54, 96, 97, 90, 121
Lamport, Charles 59
Lancaster & Carlisle Railway 10, 19, 23, 36, 145, 148
Langdale and Pikes 74, 91, 115, 128, 129-30, 132-33, 153
Leven, river and estuary 26, 29, 30, 31, 32, 39, 96

Lindal in Furness 9, 107-08
'Lion and Lamb', Grasmere 47-48, 116, 117
Little Langdale Tarn 116, 132, 134
Locomotives, British Railways 20-21, 25, 28, 43, 86-87, 108-09
Locomotives, Furness Railway 13, 14, 64, 82, 85; 'Old Coppernob' 9; No 20 15
Long Moss Tarn 127
Lonsdale, Earl of 58, 59
Loughrigg Tarn and Fell 116
Low Wood 114; gunpowder works 29, 30
Lowca Colliery 62
Lowick Bridge 113

Midland Railway 8, 9
Millom 71, 72, 73, 74; Castle 72, 74; ironworks 72, 102
Mirehouse 57
Mite, river 66, 156
Moor Row 64, 81, 82; loco shed 82
Morecambe Bay 21, 22, 24, 29, 92, 93, 106, 123
Motor yachts, see Steamers
Muncaster Castle 70-71

Nab Gill 66, 67
Nab Scar 46
Nature reserves: Blelham Bog 126; Drigg Dunes 155; Gait Barrows 22, 23; Hallsenna Moor 155;

Hodbarrow 72, 73, 149; Leighton Moss 21; Sandscale Haws 106; Warton Crag 22, 23
Nethermost Pike 48, 49
Newby Bridge 11, 29, 96, 97, 98, 144, 145
Nibthwaite 40

'Old Man of Coniston' 40, 42, 43, 44, 74, 110, 113, 123, 127
Osprey Project 57
Oxenholme 36, 37, 46

Paley, E. G. 42
Patterdale 136, 144
Penrith 51, 54, 55, 74, 76, 145-48; Castle 148
Pettigrew, William 82
Plumpton Junction 29, 96, 97, 147
Pooley Bridge 136, 145
Potter, Beatrix 89, 90, 128
Pull Wyke Bay, Windermere 128

Ramsden family 8, 101, 105
Ravenglass 66, 67, 68, 69
Ravenglass & Eskdale Railway 43, 66, 67, 73, 139, 156, 157
Red Bank 116, 118, 134
Romney, George 106
Rothay, river 48, 117, 118
Rowrah 81, 82, 83
Royal Society for the Protection of Birds (RSPB) 21, 57, 64, 72, 73, 149

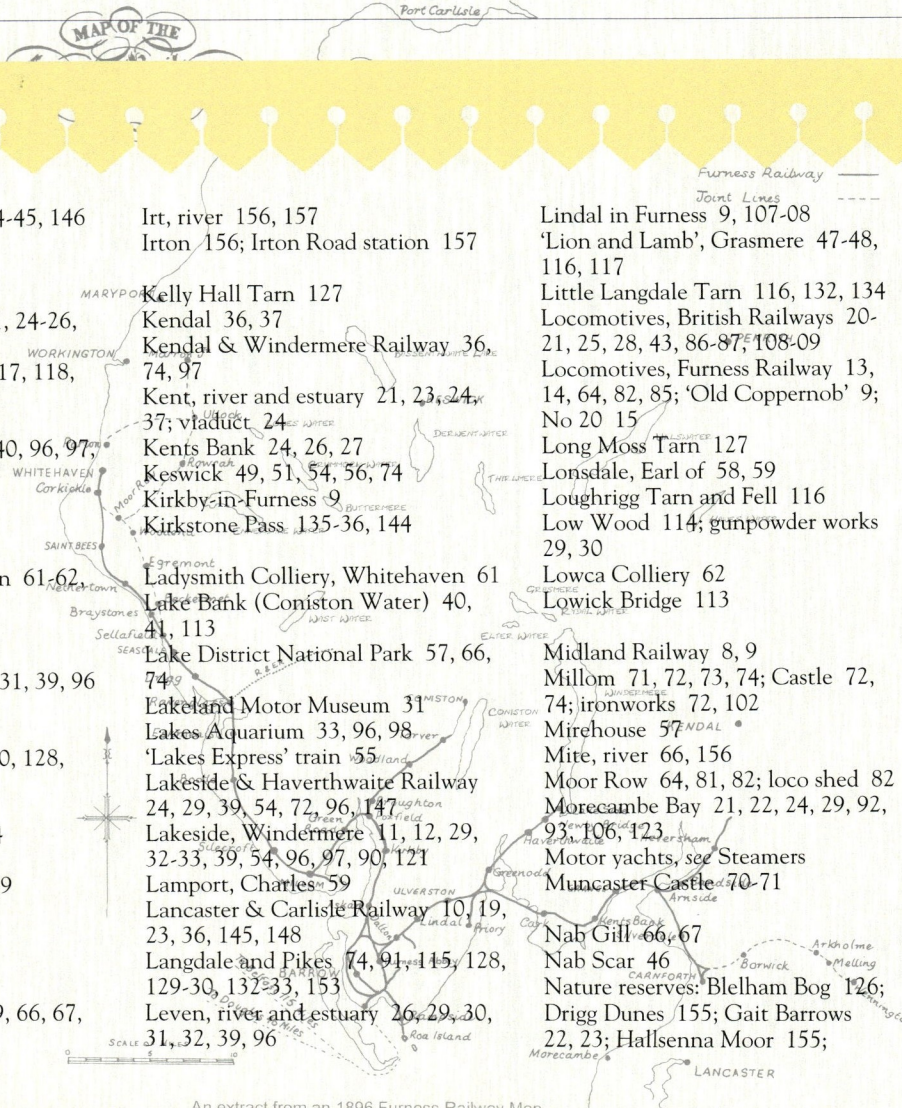

Ruskin, John 124
Rydal Water 46, 47, 117, 121

St Bees 64-65
Sandside 23, 24
Santon Bridge 156
Scafell and Scafell Pike 49, 68, 79, 141
Schneider, Henry 8, 11, 35, 102
Seascale 65, 78, 139, 154-55
Seat Sandall 48, 118
Seathwaite and Tarn 122, 151-52, 153
Sellafield and British Nuclear Fuels 22, 64, 65, 139, 155
Siddick 60, 84; St Helens Colliery 60
Silecroft 139
Silverdale 21, 22, 23
Sites of Special Scientific Interest (SSSIs) 64, 73, 91, 132, 139, 149
Skelgill 46
Skelwith Bridge 115, 118, 122, 126
Skelwith Force 116, 126, 127, 132, 133
Skiddaw 49
South Lakes Wild Animal Park 104

Stainton 11
Staveley 36
Steamers and motor yachts (lake) 17; Cygnet 34, 115; Enterprise 145; Esperance 35; Gondola 12, 41, 42, 112, 113; Lady of the Lake (1877) 145; Lady of the Lake (1907) 41, 42, 113; Raven 137, 145, 146; Swan 33, 34; Swift 34; Teal 33, 34, 115; Tern 34, 115
Steamers, Furness Railway (sea-going) 10, 13, 14, 17, 102
Steel End 118
Stickle Ghyll Tarn 134
Stock Ghyll Force 46
Storrs Hall 91
Swineside 74

Tarn Hows 91, 128, 129
Thirlmere 46, 48, 49, 75, 118, 119-20
Thirlspot 120
Threlkeld 74; Quarry & Mining Museum 74-76
Tilberthwaite 74, 112, 129
Torver 41, 42, 43, 100, 101, 109, 110-12, 113, 127
Tourism, exploited by Furness Railway 12, 55, 96-98, 143

Treacy, Eric 29
Troutbeck 74, 76, 77, 137

Ullswater 12, 49, 136, 137, 144-45, 146; Ullswater Steamers 136, 144-45
Ulpha 74, 151
Ulverston 10, 11, 21, 26-28, 54, 96, 99, 106, 122, 144; Canal 26-27, 28-29; Hoad Monument 99, 100
Ulverstone (sic) & Lancaster Railway 10, 11, 94, 102, 106

Wainwright, Alfred 37, 43, 46, 47, 49, 67, 68, 79, 112
Wansfell Pike 46
Wasdale and Wasdale Head 79, 141-42; Hall 142
Wast Water 79, 140-41
Watendlath and Tarn 119
Whitehaven 10, 60-63; Bransty station 63, 64; Corkickle Brake incline 61; Corkickle station 64 Howgill Brake incline 61
Whitehaven & Furness Junction Railway 11, 72, 74, 78, 102, 110
Whitehaven Junction Railway 60

Whitehaven, Cleator & Egremont Railway 81, 82, 84
Whitewater Hotel 31, 32 see also Backbarrow
Wilkinson, John 10
Winder 83
Windermere (lake) 12, 13, 17, 32-33, 35-36, 46, 53, 100, 128, 131, 144; ferry 88, 89, 91
Windermere (town) 35-37, 46, 97, 114
Windermere Lake Cruises 33, 39, 46, 54, 114
Windermere Steam Yacht Co 97
Woodland 42, 43, 100, 109, 110
Wordsworth, William 9, 17, 36, 47, 48, 57, 64, 74, 90, 117, 150
Workington 54, 58-60; Hall 59; port 59; shipbuilding 59
Wray Castle 126
Wrynose Pass 122, 132, 153
Wythburn 48, 119-20

Yewbarrow 141
Yewdale 74, 112, 113, 126, 129

An extract from an 1896 Furness Railway Map